Memoirs of a WWII Fighter Pilot

and some modern political commentary

KENNETH THOMPSON

Trafford rev. 06/06/2011

 www.trafford.com

North America & international
toll-free: 1 888 232 4444 (USA & Canada)
phone: 250 383 6864 ♦ fax: 812 355 4082

Chapter 1

MY YOUTH

I was born in New Munich, Minnesota on September 7, 1922. My parents were separated when I was four and my sister Marion Patricia was two. My half brother Bob was a ward of my Mother. Pat and I were boarded with the George Gibbs family until I was in the fourth grade. At that point I contracted scarlet fever and nearly died. I remember that on one night with my dad, Mr. and Mrs. Gibbs, a lady friend of my dad and the doctor all being in the room and I was floating up near the ceiling the doctor saying "If he lives the night he may pull through." I couldn't speak although I tried to but after the lights went out I started floating down a long dark tunnel. When I finally reached the end of the tunnel a shadowy figure appeared and holding a hand up while I was still in the tunnel said "go back, go back, you still have much to do." During the convalescent period following, which was fairly lengthy, I read every book in the house which included my school books, the Encyclopedia Britannica, For whom the Bells Tolled, and The Citadel among others. I went back to school about a month before the school term ended and received A's in all my subjects except deportment in which I got an F. The blonde girl who set in front of me had two long golden braids and I couldn't resist dipping her braids in the inkwell on my desk.

My dad remarried that fall to a woman named Edna Henderson and I was boarded out to her family in River Falls, Wisconsin. I was late for the start of the school year so the principal thought I should be put back in the fourth grade as in his thoughts the Wisconsin schools were ahead of the Minnesota schools and I would have a hard time catching up. I refused, so he let me enroll in the fifth grade but said they would give me a state test to see what grade I belonged in and I would have to abide by the results of that test. I agreed but stated "alright if it would be up as well as down" to which he agreed. At the mid semester brake I was called to the principals office and after much squirming the principal told me my lowest score was in math and that was the math of a twelfth grader, would I settle for the second half of the seventh grade to which I agreed. This was probably a mistake although I never had any problem academically, socially I was younger then my classmates in high school. The marriage to Edna lasted only a year, after that Pat and I lived with our grandparents in Superior, Wisconsin in the first winter and on a twenty acre farm about fifteen miles from Superior thereafter. My grandmother was a very religious person and convinced me my calling was that of the priesthood so I spent the first two years of High School in a Catholic seminary until one night I got caught reading Mill's thesis on Liberty by flashlight under the sheets and when I would not agree to read no other philosopher than St. Thomas Aquinas I was expelled.

In the meantime my dad had remarried again, this time to Adeline Sunbeck who had a home in Minneapolis. Adeline made life miserable for Pat and she wanted to leave, so I called our mother and she came up and took Pat back to Chicago with her. I had a heck of a time explaining that to dad but he finally understood. My dad had taken over a Ford dealership and garage in St. Paul. I attended Roosevelt high school in Minneapolis. My dad was an early buff of flying and had bought two airplanes, a Stinson Reliant for personal use and a Loening Amphibian which was to be flown by Pete Klimek, a friend, for a Forest Service contract. Pete however, made headlines in the Minneapolis Star Tribune when he landed in the Mississippi River with the wheels down and nosed the plane over in the water. That ended the contract. I learned to fly from another friend of my dad's by the name of Paul Meliner, a WWI ace, and I soloed at the age of thirteen. I loved to hang around the airplanes and every time my dad went out to the airport I would tag along. On one occasion dad and Pete Klimek decided they would do the 300 hour overhaul of the motor on the Stinson Reliant. I was their "go for", handling the tools they needed as they asked for them. They were imbibing as they went along finishing off a fifth of whiskey about the same time as they completed the work on the motor and feeling pretty good they decide to show me he could make a half dollar stand in the air by diving faster than the money would fall and after proving that the two of them decided to fly up to Pete's folks lodge up at the lake of the Woods, Minnesota. In 1935 I don't believe it was necessary to file a flight plan, at any rate we didn't, it was a spur of the moment decision, and off we went. Before long Pete got sleepy and moved to the back seat so he could lay down telling me to move up front and my dad to take over and what compass heading to follow. Now the Stinson has a dual set of controls and could be flown from either side. I wasn't long before we were steering off course and in looking over at my dad I could see he was fast asleep and couldn't wake him and I noticed his left foot was on the rudder so I pulled his leg off his rudder, I was in the left hand front seat and put the plane back on course. I had never had been to the lodge but I knew it was close to the juncture of The Rainy River and the Lake of the Wood, I also knew from overhearing conversations that the signal for picking Pete up was to buzz the lodge. There was no airport in the vicinity so Pete would land in some farmer's field after buzzing the lodge and on finding the lodge I did just that. The Klimeks, mother, dad and brother Paul came out to meet us and as I climbed over the farmer's fence they said where is Pete and your dad. They couldn't believe I had landed the plane and asked Paul to go look in the plane. When he looked they were both sound asleep! Paul came back later for them after they woke up. I spent the rest of the summer working for tips at the lodge, splitting woods and taking it to the guests in the cabins and waiting on tables. My dad got paranitis and everybody thought my dad was going to die, the business money vultures moved in and called all loans bankrupting the family. We moved to California. While moving into a rented house in Van Nuys, Adeline and I were arranging the furniture while my dad was at work. She wanted to move the table and I didn't understand her directions and started moving in the wrong direction. She got angry and started hitting me with a broom, unfortunately for her I grabbed a hold of the broom and having the straw end of the broom had a better grip. She fell over backwards and hit her head on the corner of the table when falling. This gave her a beautiful shiner so when my dad came home he asked her what happened. She lied and said I had hit her and my dad whirled around and socked me with a closed fist knocking me across the room. When I said I hadn't hit her he knocked me down again saying that's for lying. I went upstairs to my bedroom, tied the sheets together and dropped out the window. I didn't see my dad again until after the war. I went without food for a couple of days, but ended up in San Francisco getting a job in a parking garage while finishing high school at Polytechnic. The parking garage had a gambling room upstairs and part of my job was to ring the bell anytime a policeman came around. Another part of my job was to drive the patrons home and bring back the car and wipe it down after fog or rain got it wet. A nice looking lady customer one night told me if a gentleman came around looking for a good time I should give him her telephone number and I sent a doctor over to her. The next morning she gave me a kiss and a $5 tip. A week later I sent a lawyer to her and she told me not to send any more for a while. I only got a $2 tip that time, maybe that is the difference in value between the two, but when you are earning fifty cents an hour that seemed monstrous. At age seventeen I joined the Civilian Conservation Corps, a semi military group to save money and saved $24 a month as uniform, meals and bedding were furnished. After a few months I became an assistant leader at $36 per month and saved $30 a month. From there I got a job driving a logging truck, A Reo, hauling ten and twelve foot diameter logs down the coastal mountains onto state highway 1 until a friend ran over the cliff on the far side of the highway when he had too much speed to make the ninety degree turn. I figured there must be a better way to make a living and started looking for an engineering college. There were two engineering schools in the country that had cooperative programs where two students held one job and attended school in alternate semesters. One was Armour College of Engineering in Chicago and the other was the University of Cincinnati, I chose Armour as my mother lived there with my sister and Bob. I had saved almost $2000 and could pay for the first semester and go on the cooperative program thereafter. I worked for Wishnick-Tumpeer at their asphalt blowing plant which later became Witco Chemical Company. This was my alternate semester job. I also got part time jobs during the school year usually working in filling stations pumping gas and fixing tires on weekends. The work at Wishnick Tumpeer was in their laboratory, conducting tests on the asphalt during different stages of the blowing, stood me in good stead later in life when specifying asphalt grades for paving.

Chapter 2

WAR ON THE HORIZON

I was still 18 in June of 1941, had complete my first year of college at Armour Institute of Technology. The draft had not yet been lowered to 19 years of age but Congress was about to consider it. War had not yet broken out but we knew it was coming. My brother, Bob Thompson, was already an aviation mechanic in the navy and seeing as how I had already soloed we thought it would be a great idea to become a pilot in the Navy, that way Bob and I could team up. I would be the pilot and he my mechanic. I went to enlist and passed all the tests until I came to the dentist. The dentist failed me on the grounds that I had a malocclusion (overbite). I asked the dentist why would that eliminate me? His answer was that I would not be able to properly grip the oxygen nipple. I pointed out that I could not understand how that would eliminate me as the oxygen nipple was already passé, the navy had already gone to the oxygen mask. However. the dentist merely shook his head and said "sorry son but that's regulations." I still wanted to fly so I went across the street to enlist in the Army Air Corps. I hoped that the Air Corps didn't have the same regulation but I was leery that they might, so when the army dentist was examining my teeth, he had marked down a couple of cavities and that I had three eye teeth (I still had a baby eye tooth), he was interrupted by one of his staff members with a question and turning his back to me, answered the staff member,, then asked "where were we?" I quickly said I think we had just finished. He looked at his chart and said "Oh yes." and I went on to the next station. One other interesting thing happened during the testing. When I took the depth perception test (a test involving two small posts attached individually to strings attached to the posts and from a distance of about 15 feet align the two posts by pulling on the strings). All the people in front of me did it three times and went on to the next station. When it was my turn the examiner had me do it eight times before I asked him how many times do I have to do this? He said "until I find out how you are "cheating." Nobody is perfect eight times in a row." He had me lengthen or shorten my hold on the strings each time and even had me hold the two strings at uneven lengths. I then asked him how much the average successful candidate miss by and the answer was 3 millimeters. I then asked him where he wanted me to hold the strings and proceeded to line them up again, then pulling one a tiny bit off alignment I said there's your 3 mm and walk to the next station. When I heard him cuss I knew I had made an exact 3 mm. I passed all the physicals, signed the necessary documents and was now in the enlisted reserve for the Army Air Corp. Praise the Lord!

Chapter 3

WAR BREAKS OUT

We were still at peace so I went back to my schooling and part time job. I was in school at the time and working on weekends at the Sears Roebuck gas station at 63rd and Western. I was in my Sophomore year. I had worked the summer semester at the Wishnick-Tumpeer asphalt blowing plant as a laboratory technician. The company later became the Witco Chemical Company. On December 7, I was busy fixing a truck tire when a customer drove up to the gas pump and I went out to greet him with "How many sir?" He said "Goodbye"! I didn't' know what he was talking about and repeated, "How many?". He then said, "You haven't heard, have you?" and with that he turned up the radio. The Japs had just bombed Pearl Harbor! Then he said you are just about the right age and you'll be in the army soon. He was right. A week later I got a notice that I had thirty days notice to report to the Grand Central Railroad Station with only the clothes on my back. This was disastrous. The school semester ended the first week in February and I had to report on the evening of January 15. I studied like hell all during the Christmas holidays and then asked all my professors if I could take the finals early. I had an A or B average in all my subjects and didn't want to see the whole semester of school and my hard work wasted. All the professors refused to let me take the tests early, it was too much trouble, but the three professors of the classes that I had an A average in said I had already earned a C in their class and they would give me a C. The other two in which I had a B average volunteered D's but I said I'd rather have a drop than a D. That affected my overall grade point average. They were all heart. On January 15, 1942 I boarded the train for Miami Beach, Florida wearing only the clothes on my back as directed.

BASIC TRAINING

When I arrived at Miami Beach with a group of other reserves the Army didn't really know what our status was. We kept trying to tell them we were supposed to go to Air Corps training. They insisted we must be infantry because we were enlisted reserves and got called up. If we were to go for pilot training we would have been classified as cadets. While our status was being determined we had to go through normal basic training. We were not issued uniforms so we went through close order drill in our civilian clothes. We perspired profusely as the humidity was in the eighties.

At night the single blanket they issued us did not keep the chill off. Our clothes began to smell and it got so bad that the drill sergeant went to the Company Commander to ask that we be issue uniforms and finally we were. We must have been given special treatment as everybody got clothes and shoes that actually fit. The medical treatment however was not so good. I think most of the young doctors resented being drafted at a time they were expecting to make some money and were more interested in playing golf than treating a bunch of recruits. They were given the rank of Captain which at that time paid $200 a month. During calisthenics or obstacle course I received a green willow fracture in my lower right leg. A green willow fracture is one in which the break goes only half way through, then goes vertical down the bone for a ways. During close order drill my leg would swell up and I would start limping noticeably. The sergeant called me out of line. He looked at my swollen leg and had me sit out the rest of the drill. He told me to report to sick call in the morning, which I did. With the overnight rest the swelling went down and the doctor told me I was "gold bricking" which was a term for getting out of duty. He further stated that if I showed up on sick call again I would be put on K.P. which meant working in the kitchen. This was one of the most miserable jobs in the army. I went back to drilling (marching) with the same results, my leg swelled up once more. This time the sergeant gave me a note to give to the doctor but the following morning on sick call the doctor wouldn't even look at the note and promptly put me on K.P. I got the duty of the steam cleaner for the dishes which meant being on my feet continually all day. The army had taken over the major hotels and served thousand of soldiers, breakfast ran into lunch, a continuous stream of steel trays from 7 am to 3 pm. Then with a slight break from 4 pm to 5pm. To top everything else the mess sergeant found a speck on one of the trays we had cleaned and ordered we do all the trays over. That took care of the so called break. About 3:30 in the afternoon my sergeant came in accompanied by a major. He had suspected what the doctor had done and brought along an officer that would outrank a doctor. He asked the major to look at my leg which about this time was so swollen he had to cut the leg of my pants to see it, swore and took off to the golf course to find the doctor. In the meantime I was told to report to the doctor's office. The Major must have given the doctor quite a chewing out as the doctor was very apologetic and after looking at my leg got an immediate X-ray, put my leg in a cast which remained on my leg until we were shipped out.

When it was finally determined that we were in the Air Corps instead of sending us to cadet training Congress has decided that we needed more schooling and sent us to various schools. We embarked on a train and started North. Stops were made at Florida University, Florida A&M, Clemson, North Carolina U and State, Virginia, The Citadel and at each stop two carloads of would be cadets were dropped off. I was on the last two carloads that got off at Bluefield and then marched to Athens State Teachers College in Athens, West Virginia. As we arrive on campus shutters of the windows in the dorms flew open and girls started screaming, men, men. At first we were not allowed to commingle but the girls objected and a dance was held, but it was a girls cut.

I never got past introducing myself before another girl cut in. After a month a dozen cadets (including me) got put on report for sleeping in class. We were summoned to the Commanding Officer's office and given a severe lecture. After the lecture he asked if we had anything to say and one of the group spoke up saying "but sir, I've had a hundred on all his tests. He was quickly joined by a chorus of me to. The teacher was teaching basic high school physics and all of us had had college physics. The CO then understood why we were bored to death in his class and said we didn't belong there. He asked us to put up with the teacher for a week to ten days and he would get us into cadet training as soon as possible. True to his word, ten days later we were on our way to cadet primary.

Chapter 4

AT LAST A CADET

Just before becoming a cadet two noteworthy incidents happened. We received about an hours flying time in a Piper Cub. My instructor was a middle aged man whom I doubt had very much flying time himself. Before we took off he asked me if I had any flying experience and I informed him I had soloed. When we were airborne he told me to take over and I piloted the plane. When he told me to land I proceeded to line up with the runway and cut the throttle to glide in. Almost immediately I realized I was too high and would overshoot the runway so I started to sideslip to lose altitude in a hurry. This was a trick I had learned from the Paul Meliner, a World War I pilot, who had taught me to fly. A side slip is accomplished by lowering one wing by pushing the control stick to the left lowering the wing on the left side while simultaneously pushing in the right rudder (like a brake pedal in a car except that it makes the moveable part of the vertical stabilizer turn the nose of the airplane in the direction you push, left or right rudder). The instructor immediately grabbed the controls trying to straighten out the plane and he looked frightened. I let him take over as anyone who has flown knows that the surest way to an accident is to have two people trying to control the plane at the same time. We then aborted the landing attempt and he went around and landed the plane. On the ground he yelled at me saying I had lied about my experience as a pilot and that an experienced pilot would never cross controls. I never told anyone else that I had any previous experience after that because one never knew what limited experience the other person had and might have preconceived notions in judging you. The other item worth noting was that prior to our transfer to cadet training another student by the name of Smith and I were transferred to Newport News, issued infantry gear and boarded a transport ship bound for overseas. There we found ourselves with an infantry group that did not appear to be too literate. The only discussions going on were women and coon hunting. As the whistle blew signaling eminent departure the sergeant who had march us aboard appeared and called out Smith , Thompson, attention, leave your gear, and with that he marched us off the ship. I was the last one off and had to jump to the dock as the ship was already moving away and the gangplank was moving up. I wondered what that was all about. Later I figured that the army had minimum standards for shipment of troops overseas. Smith and I had very high scores on the army's general aptitude tests and we technically had been on board when the ship pulled out. We were there to raise the average score to an acceptable level.

Chapter 5

GROUND SCHOOL

Cadet training started with ground school. We were given tests and asked if we preferred pilot training, navigation or bombardier. I chose navigation as it would fit in with my schooling better but it was a meaningless choice. Everyone was sent to pilot training regardless of choice. If you washed out of pilot training you were sent to navigator or bombardier school. What we didn't know then that the plan was to win the war by air power and they needed thousands of pilots for this task. Ground school was fairly uneventful. Don Lawless who was later to become a tent mate and close friend was chosen by the commandant as cadet commander.

I was a corporal or squad leader. There were three platoons, each platoon having a cadet sergeant and three eleven man squads including the corporal. How they chose the cadet non commission officers I do not know. The only event that occurred of any significance was when we were awakened about three a.m. one morning to drum out two cadets for overstaying their pass and then lying about it to an officer. For a cadet to lie to an officer was a no-no so we had a white glove assembly of two parallel lines and the two were marched out between the two lines to the roll of drums never to rise above the rank of buck private for the remainder of the war.

FLIGHT TRAINING

From ground school we were sent to Dothan Field, Alabama for primary flight training. Our plane was a Steerman biplane. The landing wheels were fairly close together making it very easy to ground loop and more than one cadet was washed out for ground looping and damaging a wing as it tipped up on one wing. They were easily repaired though unless the speed had been too great when it was looped. The plane had a hand cranked inertia starter which was handled by women. They would stand on the wing and crank until it had sufficient speed to engage the motor then jump off. One of the cadets married one of the women who cranked the inertia starter. It turned out she had a venereal disease that was incurable and when he would not divorce her he was discharged. I was the first to solo, which was hardly a surprise, seeing as how I had soloed before entering the army. I hadn't told anyone at the base that I had previously flown so I guess they thought I was a fast learner or a natural. After soloing one of the tasks we had to perform was a cross country flight. We were to fly to Memphis, Tennessee on the first leg of the cross country, then to Little Rock, Arkansas, then back home to Dothan. I got pretty bored with the trip so just outside of Little Rock I decided to fake an emergency landing. I cut the throttle rapidly several times then cut the throttle completely faking engine trouble. Picking out a likely looking farmer's field I made a perfect three point landing.

The farmer came running over and said he had heard the sputtering engine and knew I had had an emergency and guided me back to the house where I could call base on the telephone and report. My orders were I was not to attempt to fix the plane and stay where I was, they would send a mechanic the following day. The farmer was very gracious putting me up for the night and feeding me a sumptuous dinner and breakfast, the best I had while in the service. The following day two planes arrived, one with a pilot and a mechanic and the other with just a pilot. The mechanic was also a pilot so when we took off to go back to Dothan I was just a passenger in the plane piloted by the company commander. When the mechanic could find nothing wrong with the plane the Commanding Officer questioned the farmer who backed my story of engine trouble but added suspicion by telling the CO That I had made a better landing than either of the pilots who came in that morning. While having a cup of rationed coffee at the farmer's home he questioned the wife of the farmer even asking her maiden name but could find no relationship between us. When we got back to base he questioned me thoroughly about my possible relationship to the farmer but I truthfully told him I had never seen the farmer before and was not a relative. He suspected that I had faked the landing just to visit relatives but it never occurred to him that I would fake an emergency landing just to break the boredom of the cross country. I was off the hook. One other instance happened that affected my life thereafter. I had bought a graduation ring from the Post Exchange after being informed I had graduated. On my last solo flight after I finished my acrobatics I put the plane into a tail spin. When attempting to pull out my ring finger got caught in the throttle quadrant and I could not add throttle. Just before I stalled out again I managed to free my finger, a little bloodied but free to add throttle and avoid a crash. I took the ring off, threw it overboard and never wore a ring again. Not even a wedding ring!

Chapter 6

ON TO BASIC FLIGHT SCHOOL

The next stop was at a field in Mississippi whose name I do not remember where we flew a low wing metal aircraft made by Vultee which we knew as the Vultee vibrator. The Steerman had been a bi-wing, fabric covered aircraft which after the war was modified to become a crop duster. Both planes had fixed wheel landing gear. My instructor was a gentleman named Gatlin who had a profound influence on my future. We did about the same routine in flying as we had in primary but this time I didn't make a fake motor trouble landing. Besides, the plane was faster and didn't take as long. Instead I satisfied my boredom with a few barrel and slow rolls along the way.

Just before I graduated from basic he told me I was one of the best pilots he had ever trained and on graduation day he came up to me and said "You would rather fly fighters than push box cars around wouldn't you?. Box cars was his reference to multi engine bombers, I've recommended you for single engine advance. I was overjoyed! It's much more fun to fly a plane one can move around and do acrobatics with than flying straight and level. He started to walk away, when in an after thought he turned back and said "Oh by the way, I had to change your height, if your over 5' 10" tall you have to go to twin engine advance."

The next day the loud speaker blared out "Cadets Sullivan, Thompson, report to the CO's office." We reported together and the commanding officer immediately pointed a finger at Sullivan and said "which one are you?" Sullivan was 5' 6" tall and was immediately excused with the CO saying "I can see you really are 5' 6", your physical training record said 6' 5"." Then he turned to me and said "and how tall are you Mr. Thompson?" I was in a quandary, if I lied I would be drummed out of the air corps and if I told the truth I would have to go to twin engine advance. So I said I don't rightly know sir but I'm close to six foot". He then said he could see that, "Six foot what?" I slumped a little from my six foot two frame and replied "Oh I wouldn't say that sir". "What would you say?" "Close to six foot, sir." We bandied back and forth for a short time and I never did admit my height was 6'2" so finally he sent me up to the doctor to be measured saying "No more bandying of words Mr. Thompson, we will abide by the doctor's findings." I hadn't lied and I never admitted being over six foot tall. The doctor was an elderly man and busier than heck giving physicals to a bunch of new recruits when he turned to me asking what I wanted. I explained what had happened at the CO's office and that I'd like to go to single engine advance. He just smiled and said "Can you get under that?" pointing to a scale with the height bar extended. He didn't say I couldn't duck so I replied in the affirmative. He walked over to the scale and read the height and marked down on the paper four foot ten inches. When I questioned the doctor saying the CO would never believe that, the doctor just said "you tell him I'm the doctor around here." As soon as I got back to the office I handed the CO the paper on which my bogus height was written and signed by the doctor. He then said without looking at the paper "Now we'll no longer have this bandying of words and abide by the doctor's findings won't we?" I then replied "I hope so sir." Puzzled by my answer he opened the folded paper and jumping straight up out his chair exclaimed "four foot ten", then he started laughing saying I was a better talker than the doctor was a doctor, but an agreement is an agreement and signed my papers for single engine advance. And that is how, despite my height I ended up in fighters.

Chapter 7

SINGLE ENGINE ADVANCE

Napier Field, Alabama was the next stop and the last stop before becoming commission officers in the Army Air Corps with silver wings et al. The plane we flew was a low wing metal aircraft with retractable landing gear, cruised at 160 miles an hour and was the sweetest ship I ever flew. I sure would have liked to have one after the war. Don Lawless, Eugene Van Houten and myself started hanging out together and were to become tent mates overseas. On my days off instead of chasing women in the small town near the field I would go to the golf course or the skeet range. There must have been at least 100 service men for every young woman in that town and I saw no point in going there. One time at the golf course as I was about to tee off an officer came up and asked if he could play along. He had no clubs and I expected him to go into the clubhouse and get some but instead he asked me if I used my two wood much and when I said no, he asked if he could borrow it. He then asked me if I had an old ball he could borrow and I lent him one. He must have been a pro as he shot a 72 using that two wood for driving, fairway shots, chipping and putting while I shot in the eighties using a full bag of clubs. I never did get his name but often wondered after the war if he was on the pro circuit. I was a good shot with a shotgun and did well on the skeet range from the various stations. I shot twenty five out of twenty five on many occasions. The toughest shot was the set of doubles shot from the center station. The flying routine was again pretty much the same with night landings added to the curriculum and more emphasis placed on maneuvers. At any rate there were no washouts at Napier Field and we all graduated. We had previously ordered our officers uniforms which we had to pay for out of our cadet salaries ourselves. Just before we graduated they shaved the hair off our heads. This is why newly commissioned lieutenants are called shave tails. The hats we had ordered when we had a full head of hair now dropped down to the ears. Then we were given a week leave before reporting to Harris Neck, Georgia. I visited my mother and sister in Chicago, Illinois, then reported.

Chapter 8

HARRIS NECK, GEORGIA

After getting my commission I received my fighter plane training at Harris Neck Georgia. There we flew an early version of the P-40 Curtis Tomahawk made famous by the Flying Tigers. The cockpit was tight but livable as my head touched the canopy. Harris Neck was an isolated area just South of Savannah. Here stray bullets and bombs could do little damage. I received an expert rating in both aerial gunnery and dive bombing. Aerial gunnery consisted of a tow plane towing a target banner some distance behind the plane and the percentage of holes in the target of the shots you fired determined your accuracy. For some ungodly reason our night landing qualification was done in the P-39 Bell Aircobra, a tricycle landing gear craft and we were given no flight time in it for familiarization. If one landed nose wheel first you stood a good chance of buckling the wheel and wrecking the plane. To top matters off the night chosen for night landings was overcast and the entire coast was under the strictest blackout because of Nazi U-boats patrolling our coast and were sinking our merchant ships. The landing field was dimly lit with flares and unless you had those flares in sight the only way one could tell which way was up was by the feel in the seat of your pants and the instrument panels artificial horizon. On top of all that the cockpit was small and cramped, a 75mm canon ran between the pilot's legs and the distance between the seat and the canopy was so short I couldn't close the canopy and get my head up over a 45 degree angle to see over the engine. I flew with canopy open, looked over the top of the windshield, relied on my goggles to protect my eyes from the wind and said a few prayers that night making the three landings necessary to qualify. Some pilots had to make five or six landings before they qualified. I was happy to have gotten off with three and hoped to never fly a P-39 again. My wish was granted as the government decided to sell all the P-39s to the Russians and they never saw action as a U.S. war plane to my knowledge.

Every officer had to qualify on the M-1 rifle, the Thompson sub machine gun and the Colt 45 automatic. I had no difficulty qualifying on the M-1 or the Thompson sub machine gun although an amusing thing happened on the Thompson sub machine gun. On the M-1 I qualified as a sharpshooter and on the Thompson I got an expert rating, the highest rating scoring 25 out of 25 with one bullet in the heart in each of the twelve pop up targets. You would walk down a path and a cardboard image of a man would pop out from behind a tree or building and you were supposed to put two bullets in each one and three in the last one shooting from the hip. My second shot in each case was in the center of the inscribed heart. One of the other fellows afterwards asked if I was a relative of the Thompson who invented the sub machine gun and with a straight face I answered yes, he was my old man. The other officer then said "No wonder, I thought there had to be a reason you were so good." The truth was my grandfather had taught me how to shoot a .410 shotgun from the hip shooting at ground squirrels. I didn't do so well on the 45. I had never shot a revolver in my life and on my third and last qualifying try the sergeant started off by saying let me show you how. He then fired two shot into the target, then handed the revolver to me and said go ahead. I fired two shots and missed, he then grabbed the gun saying no, no. It's like this, he then fired three shots and handed the gun back to me. When I attempted to fire the gun just clicked; it was empty. He then looked at the target and said, five out of seven, not bad lieutenant, you qualify, all this with an absolutely straight face. I received a marksman rating, the lowest of the three qualifying grades. The army was in desperate need of pilots and they were not about to disqualify anyone because they couldn't hit the broadside of a barn with that 45. Several other pilots had the same experience.

After a month of training in fighters we were ready for action. We sailed from Newport Beach, Virginia. The ship left at night with no lights to sneak pass the U-boat blockade. Once on the open sea it relied on its speed to avoid the enemy. The ship carried about twenty nurses, a couple hundred pilots, a few hundred ground crew officers on the upper deck and around one thousand ground crew personnel on the lower deck. The ship captain decided there were too many officers for the officer's lounge and had the pilots locked in the hold. The hold was our sleeping quarters with hammocks for beds. Several pilots got seasick with dire results. The hold soon reeked with the odor of vomit. When gunnery practice was held and we didn't know whether or not we were being attacked, it didn't help tempers any. On the fourth day the captain decided to hold inspection and got quite a surprise, he and the mate were staring at a dozen or more Colt 45s. After some brief negotiations in which he agreed that attempting to court marshal two hundred officers was a bad idea, that we needed fresh air and the right to walk on deck in exchange for his well being was a better idea, we were freed. The rest of the trip was uneventful and we got to see the Straits of Gibraltar as we passed through and the Isle of Capri which shelters Naples Harbor where we disembarked.

Chapter 9

SQUADRON ASSIGNMENT

Thirteen of us were assigned to the Eighty Fifth Fighter Squadron of the Seventy Ninth Fighter Group which had recently come up from Africa where they had served under Montgomery of the British Eighth Army. However they were now assigned to the American Third Army. We were the first replacements to go to the 79th and most of the pilots already had sixty five to seventy-five missions under their belts. After we were assigned quarters we were given liberty as the weather was damp and foggy and there would be no flying weather for the next few days. Don Lawless, Eugene Van Houten and I decided to check out a jeep and explore Naples. Naples was a mix of very old homes, some dating back to Roman times and very new and modern buildings. The old homes were mostly on cobblestone narrow streets while the newer ones were on asphalt paved wide streets. The newer areas also had sewers where the accepted practice in the older sections was overnight pots which were emptied onto the street where the refuse was washed down into the bay. Where there were more than one story buildings a person walking down the street had to keep a watchful eye upwards. Mussolini's great claim was that he made the trains run on time and established sewers in the more modern sections of Italy. We hadn't been traveling too long before we got flagged down by a frantically waving man. When we stopped we found out that he wanted to be our guide around Naples. At first we weren't interested until he started waving some papers at us shouting "me no damned foreigner, me Americano." We looked at his papers and sure enough, he had the first papers for American citizenship. It seems he had taken out the first papers and had gone back to Italy to show his relatives and got caught there when the war with the States broke out. He asked where each of us was from, at first I told him Palo Alto where my dad lived and he failed to recognize the whereabouts of Palo Alto, I told him San Francisco He said "Then you know my brother Luigi, he lives there." He had no idea of the size of San Francisco. We then hired him to help him out and each of us gave him a hundred Lire note in occupation money and he was so grateful he guided us to Pompeii where the Italian government had started excavation of that city which had been buried in volcanic ash for several centuries. It turned out to be a very interesting trip. I was particularly interested in the soldiers armor which I had at first thought was for children. It would not have fit anyone over five feet tall. When he said no, it was for the regular Roman soldiers of that time. I then thought of the Movie BEN HUR where the principle characters were played by six foot four Charles Hesston and six foot three Robert Boyd. They would have been Goliaths in Roman times. The homes were built around a courtyard the roofs of which funneled rain runoff into large vases. Only a few blocks had been excavated at that time. By the time we had examined everything it was time to get back to our bivouac area and chow. The Eighty Fifth Fighter Squadron was already converting to the P-47 Thunderbolts. A radial engine fighter plane with eight fifty caliber machine guns mounted in the wings. They were the razorback model of the A, B and C variety but no "bubble-jobs." They were not to be issued to us until when we were at the Serragio base on Corsica. I believe I was the only new recruit to fly a mission from Capodichino. The primary duty of the Seventy Ninth Fighter Group at that time was to cover the Anzio beachhead. We flew cover for the ships landing supplies and the ground troops already on shore. We also patrolled the Appian Way destroying any German motor transports we could find. Capopdichino was a very busy airport with several outfits flying out of it after the Vesuvius eruption made every airport in the vicinity inoperable except Capodichino.

Chapter 10

SOMEONE UP THERE WAS WATCHING OUT FOR ME

From Capadichino we moved to a newly constructed air base at Serragia, Corsica about 20 miles south of Bastia, Corsica in order to cover both the Anzio beachhead and southern France. We had just completed putting up our own tent and finished work on the tent that was to be the officers club when after breaking in the bar with a few drinks someone suggested we check out a jeep and explore the island. Seven of us started down the west coast highway to the first town indicated on the map and found it to be only a few scattered houses. Further inquiry indicated that the next town was no different and that there were only two towns of any significance and they were Bastia on the northeast side of the island and Ajaccio on the southwest side. It was getting dark. The jeep had tape over the lights so that only a narrow slit of light was projected on the roadway. This was in accordance with blackout regulations. The officer who had been driving suggested that I take over the driving as I was the soberest in the group. I probably held my liquor better than most due to the high red corpuscle count I had had ever since I had worked at logging in the mountains. At any rate I took over the driving and turned back north to the road that crossed over the mountains to the East side highway to Ajaccio. I had only gone a short distance on this road when the area in front of me seemed unusually dark so I stopped to investigate why. Everyone climbed out when I explained why I had stopped and we walked forward to see why it appeared darker on ahead. We only went about a hundred feet when we were looking at a bombed out bridge and a very dark chasm. Had we continued on we would have plunged off into a canyon several hundred feet below. The rest of the officers, who had been singing and pounding the sides of the jeep moments before, had followed me to see why I had stopped. They were suddenly very quiet and instantly sober. I do not know why I stopped but six of my comrades and I were very grateful that I had. Someone up there must have been watching!

The following morning we got down to business. None of us had ever flown a P-47 Thunderbolt, all our previous training had been in Curtis P-40s except for our night flying which had been done in P-39s. Major Martin was our commanding officer and he had over 100 combat missions. The outfit had received some nice new P-47 Ds which were bubble jobs, that is the canopy was a bubble that gave you 360 degree visibility. The A, B and C models were called razorbacks and went straight back from the top of the windshield to the tail assembly. The so called "bubble-jobs" had a Plexiglas bubble sitting on top of the fuselage. The razor back had limited visibility behind. I was assigned a new P-47 D model. As soon as I sat in the cockpit I loved the P-47, it had room galore. The P-40 was a very tight squeeze and the 39 was impossible for a man of my height (six foot two) to be an effective pilot. We were given two hours flying time to familiarize ourselves with the characteristics of the airplane which was not much time before we took it into combat. I made the most of my time. A fighter plane has only room for one person in the cockpit so there is no one along to help you out, and there is a lot to learn. There were over a dozen instruments on the panel plus switches controlling your inertia starter, cowling flaps, gun sight, lights, IFF, tail wheel lock, etc. To hit the wrong one at the wrong time could be fatal. I took the plane up to twenty thousand feet and started to wring it out. The first thing was to try stalls power on and power off. The IFF switch was identification, friend or foe, it put a blip on the radar screen so our own anti air craft batteries wouldn't shoot at us if we returned to base after dark. I immediately discovered that the rudder controls were lost first and the aileron controls last. This was the exact opposite of what we had been taught in conventional aircraft! The bubble canopy was causing a whirling of the air behind the bubble which in turn caused the loss of a smooth air flow over the elevators and rudder which caused the loss of control there first. This was important to know! I next tried barrel rolls and a slow roll. When the airplane was upside down the engine quit. The carburetor was a gravity feed and upside down no fuel was fed to the engine. This of course could have been learned by reading the specification manual if we had been furnished one but we were not. On landing I immediately demanded one. From that I also learned what speeds gave a no load situation on the tail which later contributed to saving my life and also the self sealing main gas tank which later contributed to saving Kretzer's life. I then tried an Immelmann, a half loop and half roll but stalled out at the top, not completing the half roll and went into a flat spin upside down. I fell approximately fifteen thousand feet before the nose dropped

P-47E Thunderbolt

P47D Thunderbolt

of enough to cause an airflow over the ailerons enabling me to right the plane and restart the engine. When I finally pulled out I was at two thousand feet above the sea. Glancing at my watch I saw my two hours were up and went back to our air base at Serragia. That night at a meeting with the commanding officer and the other pilots I reported my findings on the stall characteristics and was immediately greeted by a loud round of guffaws. Major Martin came to my rescue saying my record showed I was a pretty good pilot and he would check it out in the morning. He then told me if I was correct I should prepare a letter to Republic Aircraft for his signature telling them of my findings. The following day he checked out my findings and as soon as he got back to the shack he used as an office, he found my letter sitting on his desk for his signature. After reading it he looked up at me and said "pretty sure of yourself weren't you", he then picked up a pen and signed it. As a result when the P-47 E model came out correcting this problem I received the first one to be delivered to our outfit and our squadron received the first batch of the E model. The correction was the addition of a Dorsal fin beginning at the back of the bubble and going back to the rudder slightly higher as it went to a height of about fifteen to eighteen inches. This kept enough of the airflow flowing over the rudder and elevators to avoid the adverse effects in a stall. In the mean time all flew the P-47 D which soon replaced all the A, B, and C models although 86 and 87 squadrons flew some modified versions of the C model to the very end.

I was soon to be assigned my own plane, X-37, the very first E model and I rushed down to the revetment where it was parked to find my crew chief busily painting my name and rank along with his name and rank and that of the armorer. To my dismay his rank was buck private and the armorer was corporal. Now crew chiefs were supposed to be staff sergeants. To be outranked by the armorer was an impossible situation, how can crew chief be in charge of the maintenance of the plane when the armorer outranked him. I couldn't believe it! The stupidity of the brass! I was immediately angry and turning on my heel I dashed up to the operations officer, Major Mullins, by name, and started to raise hell. I found out that it had been the policy of the outfit to raise the ranks of the non-commissioned officers based on their longevity overseas and not on their position, that there were several crew chiefs who were privates. I threaten to go over the heads of our outfit to correct this situation. Major Mullins then asked me to calm down and looked over his chart of non-coms and told me he had one opening for a corporal and if that would satisfy me he would give that to my crew chief and that he would give my crew chief the first sergeants rating that came open. Knowing that it would take six months or more to go through channels I accepted. I then went back to my plane and told Ed Hollywood, my crew chief, to erase that private and make it corporal. He protested but I told him that's an order and if he didn't believe me to read the bulletin board in the morning. It was the start of beautiful friendship and Hollywood was the most totally loyal crew chief in the squadron.

After the move to Corsica our first mission was dive bombing and strafing on the harbor and island of Elbe where Napoleon had been imprisoned after his defeat at Waterloo. The mission had little significance other than a training mission for the Free French forces on invasion tactics. The mission however was an awakening for us, Lt Green, one of my tent mates, was killed when he flew his plane into the target. I believe it was due to inadequate training in the P-47. He was the first of six tent mates that were lost. However two of them returned alive, Van Houten who was picked up by the Italian partisans and never captured and Bell who was a prisoner of war when he was shot down after twelve missions.

The main purpose of the 79th move to Corsica was to shorten the distance we had to fly to cover the Anzio beach head and to allow us to attack targets in Vichy France (the southern part of France left under French civilian control) although the Germans occupied the military posts and aerodromes. Before we could invade southern France we had to be able to soften up these military posts and destroy their local air power.

X37, my plane with Captain Lawless standing in front of the plane

Chapter 11

MA, THEY ARE SHOOTING AT ME

Around the beginning of July about two weeks after we had become operational the brass decided we were ready to raid an airdrome in Southern France. The plan was for 85 squadron to strafe the airfield while 87 squadron flew cover then when we had made several passes 85 squadron would fly cover for 87 squadron. We each had twelve airships. I flew tail end Charlie in yellow flight. Each flight had four ships, Dickie leader, red flight and yellow flight. Yellow flight always flew off sun to better protect the squadron in case we were jumped by enemy aircraft. We went straight in and I picked out a JU-88 bomber and started it ablaze. By the time I came around for the second pass the German gunners were all primed and as I started opening fire I was hit in both wings and as I passed the field I got hit in the tail section. I immediately kept my altitude just above tree top level to make myself as little of a target as possible and assessed the damage. My vertical stabilizer was half shot off and a hole in my left wing had a hole in it big enough to crawl through with a gun belt streaming out in the wind and a hole in my right wing about eighteen inches in diameter. I reduced my airspeed to give me zero stress on the tail section and made a slow turn to the south keeping the plane at treetop level. I also noted that I was leaking oil from the top cylinders as the oil was coming out fairly slowly from beneath the cowling flaps on the top but not enough to destroy my forward vision. It took forever to reach the Mediterranean which was my objective. I thought once I reached a comfortable distance off shore I could crash land and the navy could pick me up. About that time I looked up to my left and saw our planes on their way back to Corsica. The motor was still running alright and the plane was still flying so I thought I might be able to get back to Serragia. I then started gentle climb and turn to head home. I could not keep up with our planes as I was flying at

32

about one hundred and sixty mph whereas normal cruising in a P-47 was two hundred thirty mph indicated. Actual air speed was 2% higher for every thousand feet of altitude you were above the ground. As I neared Corsica my temperature gauge was climbing and by the time I notified the control tower that I was coming in, my engine was overheated and I would come straight in. My temperature gauge had hit the end of the red zone. I was afraid to cut the throttle for fear the engine wood quit and I was right. I made a hot landing and didn't cut the throttle until I was about one hundred feet from the front end of the runway and as soon as I cut the throttle the engine froze and the propeller stopped. I used the whole runway riding my brakes as much as I dared to deep from nosing over. Afterwards my crew chief asked me why I hadn't bailed out. I told him first off I was to low when over France and I didn't want to spend the war in a German prisoner camp, additionally When I got over the open sea I didn't want to get wet, besides if I could bring the plane back it could be salvaged for parts. "What parts?" he asked. "The engine was fused together, the wings had big holes in them, the rudder was half shot off, the elevators had holes in them and the tires were worn bald. I ask "what about the prop?" Hollywood shook his head in disgust and walked off. One thing I was sure of, the P-47 was one hell of a rugged airplane. The truth of the matter is it never occurred to me to bail out as long as I had control of the plane.

Chapter 12

CAPRI REST LEAVE

After about twenty missions Don Lawless and I went on rest leave together on the Isle of Capri. Some pilots got rest leave in Rome but we had no choice. We were dropped off at a hotel and were immediately greeted with a rowdy scene. A nurse, who obviously had quite a few drinks, had a pair of scissors with which she promptly snipped off our ties, yes, we wore ties, before we had ordered our first drink. Then she told the bartender to give us two more because we were behind the rest before she moved on to greet the next arrival with her sheers. After finishing my drinks I went up to our assigned room and went to sleep. I slept soundly and do not know when Don came to bed. The next morning we went on tour and visited the blue grotto which was a cave that could only be entered by boat and gave off a blue fluorescent glow. The wave action had an up and down motion in the cave and coupled with an excessive amount of alcohol the night before made Don sick. He retired back to our bedroom but I went on to see the Tiberian castle which was built for the Roman Emperor Tiberius. I marveled at the roadway which had been hacked out of the sheer cliff on the West side of the island and wondered how many slaves had lost their lives making that road. I also visited the Catholic Church in the town of Antecapri on the Northerly tip of the island which had some astounding mosaics. The town of Capri is mainly a fishing village but did have the hotel we stayed at for tourists. After a few days we returned to base on Corsica. It was the last time Don and I were on leave together as the powers that be decided we could not be spared at the same time. Don was the first of our group to be promoted to Captain, probably because he had been group commander when we were cadets. By now Don and I were both in charge of our flights when on missions.

Chapter 13

INVASION OF VICHY, FRANCE

In August of 1944 our troops invaded Southern France. On D Day, I had a four ship patrol that had two pill boxes as a target. The pill box was a concrete cylinder housing German guns meant to turn back any invading force. We were to take off at 3 a.m. It was pitch black out with the stars very dim due to a humidity haze. We were to rendezvous at five thousand feet then proceed to target

My wingman promptly joined me, I had my wing lights on so I could be found, However my Element leader never did join up, after about ten minutes I called to him to tell him I was heading out on course but he said he had me in sight. I was just above him. I asked him his altitude and he told me thirteen thousand. At that point I informed him he was looking at a star. I was at five thousand and would climb to ten thousand on my way to the target and gave him a course to steer. We never did join up. As dawn broke there were quite a few single airplanes around, one a P-47 with French markings asked if I had a target and could he join up with me. Also an 86 or 87 pilot who had lost his leader asked to join so we ended up with four ships and tried to knock out the pill boxes. We shook them up a bit with near misses but no direct hits, but the navy artillery took care of them. The air over the beachhead was filled with planes, over two hundred in all, and when commander informed us forty bandits (German aircraft) were headed our way. Commander was the ground controller and in this case was probably located on one of the Navy ships where radar had picked up the German planes. Every one of those two hundred planes eagerly turned north to greet them. The Germans then thought better of it and high tailed it for home. We stayed in the target area until our gas ran low, shooting up any truck or tank that moved, then returned to base.

Chapter 14

SEARCH AND DESTROY

After the invasion of Southern France we had many missions of plain old search and destroy. These were usually four ship shows where continuous coverage of certain sectors was important. On one such mission Captain Cronk caught the German Army in full retreat from the beachhead and without telling any other outfit had 85th squadron patrols one after another cover his sector. From dawn to dusk one patrol after another emptied their guns on the German convoy literally blocking the road with destroyed vehicles of every type, from trucks and armored vehicles to horse drawn wagons. I was later to view this carnage from the ground. As a matter of fact I picked up a motorcycle and a German P38 Lugar revolver from there. It took a bulldozer to clear over a 30miles of this debris. Bodies, trucks, wagons, tanks and what have were shoved into a trench and buried.

During the months of August and September our outfit destroyed over 400 trucks, 20 locomotives, 200 rail cars, thirty aircraft on the ground, 100 horses, 20 bridges, 50 gun positions, 5 tanks and numerous buildings. The P-47 Thunderbolt was an effective weapon of war. By the end of September targets were getting too far away. I was the first to get a target that was so far away we did not have enough gas to get back to Corsica. We were to land at the Valence airdrome which our forces were supposed to have under control. This was the same airdrome in which I had been shot up badly in an earlier describe mission. As we were approaching the field in preparation to landing a Folke-Wolf 190 was taking off. One of the fellows said shall we get him. I had already seen the 190 and decided not to get him but I replied "look at your gas gauge, if you've got enough left get him, I'm on empty." He would have been a sitting duck but none of us had enough fuel left and it would make no sense to get him, then, crash land yourself because you do not have enough gas left to make it back to land at the airdrome. That was one lucky Hun! As we came in for a landing I saw gun flashes as I passed the tower, so I rolled on to the far end of the runway and pulled off. The four of us assembled there and listened to the gun fighting that was going on in the tower and barracks area. One of the guys asked "what are we doing here" my reply was listen to that gun fire down by the control tower, this field was supposed to have been under the control of the 3rd Army. We decided then to walk into town, a couple of miles distance and see what gives. Our briefing before we left had told us the airdrome was secure. As we came into town people began gathering in the streets and started cheering us. We were the first Americans they had seen. We were greeted as liberators! The army had bypassed Valence and failed to notify our headquarters. They had left the capture of the airfield up to special operations, a secret group which supplied the French resistance forces with weapons and targets. The undercover French force had gone out to secure the airdrome and that was what the shooting was all about that had been going on when we landed. The townspeople were more than willing to feed us supper and share a bottle of wine. After dark we headed back to the airdrome and came to a fork in the road which none of us had noticed on the way in. While we were discussing which fork to take a voice came out with a distinct British accent "Oh I say there chaps, are you looking for the airdrome, take the fork to the right." He then approached us knowing we were the pilots of the P-47s that had landed that afternoon. He explained that he was a member of the FFI, in short the underground fighting force that had just captured the airdrome from the Germans who had been left behind. They took no prisoners. The Germans would have been better off if they could have surrendered to an American force. The next day our ground crew arrived with supplies and I swiped a gallon can of bully beef and gave it to the family that I had supper and a bottle of clarinet with. They insisted I have dinner with them and bully beef never tasted that good at any other time. The next day I took the ten year old boy and thirteen year old girl out to see the planes and look in the cockpit of my plane. Hundreds of townspeople came out to view our planes at this open house. The boy was thrilled when I let him sit in the cockpit of my plane. I'll bet he was the envy of every boy in Valence. The girl was a little shocked when she saw the name on one of the other planes, The La Fongool and I let you imagine what that meant in French. After a couple of hour I took the kids and another can of bully beef back to the mother. Their father was in the resistance and had been killed by the Germans. After a short time we were once again reaching the limit of our range. It was on one such mission that while skip bombing a German tank I took a hit in my gas tank. Although the fuel tank was self sealing I had lost enough fuel so that I could not make it back to our base. I told the rest of the squadron to proceed back to base and I would throttle back to maximum fuel efficiency and get back as far as I could. When the engine started sputtering I quickly picked out an open field and bellied the plane in coming to a halt about a hundred yards from a roadway. I knew I was in friendly territory so when I got out of the plane and started toward the road I saw a women frantically jumping up and down. I stopped and heard her shouting "minen, minen". I WAS IN A MINE FIELD! I froze on the spot. She ran off to the east and came back about two hours later with two Scottish soldiers with a mine detector. The Scotsman told me to follow his footprints exactly and there was but one set of footprints coming out of that field. I can truthfully say that I was never scared on any mission, I was always too busy planning my mission, looking around for targets and enemy aircraft to be scared but I was scared walking out of that minefield. I was afraid of coming back a cripple and German mines were not intended to kill, only maim.

Chapter 15

SOB STORY

I returned late one night from a poker game to our tent to hear a sobbing sound coming from within. The tent was now occupied by only two pilots, Don Lawless and me. We had lost Gene Van Houten on his twenty-sixth mission. Don had taken Van's loss rather hard as the three of us had gone all the way through pilot training together. I had taken their picture together at a table outside a restaurant in Bastia. That picture later showed up in a book on the Seventy Ninth Fighter Group by Don Woerpel. All of the losses had occurred in order around the tent starting at my foot with Lt. Green, then Ramsdell, Harding, Bell and Van Houten on his twenty-sixth mission. When I first entered the tent and found Don sobbing I had thought he had some bad news from home but this did not turn out to be the case. The next day he was to fly his thirty-third mission and he somehow got the notion it was his turn to be killed. I tried my best to dissuade him but could not. Finally I offered to trade places in the tent with him and he was overjoyed at the prospect. However I told him I would only exchange places with him if he would agree, along with me, that we would stay overseas until the war was won. I made this a condition because I thought that at least three of the other casualties had been caused by the fellows thinking of going home rather on concentrating on winning the war. Don readily agreed and neither of us thought about returning home until the war in Europe was over. We also refused to take any more tent mates and for a long time the brass honored our feelings on this. Much later in the war we had to take another tent mate, Lt. McHenry by name and we lost him but not until he had sixty-eight missions. I still have a hard time fathoming his loss. In leading well over sixty missions, he was the only man I ever lost while leading a mission. On the mission I lost him, I was Dickie leader and he was my element leader. We had successfully

Ken Thompson

completed our mission, was over the Adriatic Sea at about twelve thousand feet, when I looked over at him and he gave me an A O.K. sign. I looked the other way seeing that the sky was clear of enemy aircraft and looked back in his direction. He was nowhere to be seen! I called his name and got no answered. I asked the other pilots where he was and the answer was his plane just disintegrated. Why, no one knew. His plane just came apart all at once. To this day I think about it and always come up with the same question, why? Why? Why! At any rate after exchanging places with our cots Don ended up with one hundred missions and I ended up with ninety six missions. I had lost a few days after I was shot done behind enemy lines because it had taken me about ten days to walk back.

Chapter 16

BRON AIRDROME

We flew only a few missions from the Bron airdrome. Early morning fog and short days limited our flying time. At every station in France however, we were billeted in buildings as opposed to the tents at Serragio and later in Italy. Lyon was a large enough city that it had some fine restaurants and quite a few of the pilots, myself included, chose to spend our flying pay on eating out. Once a month we received rations of cigarettes, whiskey, candy, and cigars. I never smoked cigarettes so I would trade a pack of cigarettes for two cigars, one month allotment of cigars. We got a carton of cigarettes and a bottle of whiskey (the whiskey went straight to the officers club). On one month there were no cigars, nothing to trade for so I gave a pack to the orchestra leader at a restaurant when entering, and he asked me what my favorite song was. I told him "18th Century Drawing Room" which the orchestra promptly played. From that time on every time I entered that restaurant the orchestra would promptly start playing 18th Century Drawing Room. Some times in times of war nice thing, memorable things happen. Three of us pilots went out to dinner, the other two had dates with some local girls and they suggested a very nice restaurant that had an orchestra and dance floor. The only dance step I was any good at was the waltz and while the orchestra was playing the Blue Danube waltz I spotted a nice looking young lady having dinner with her parents. As was the custom in the finer families of France I asked her father for permission to ask the young lady for a dance which was granted. We were the only couple on the dance floor and we did a couple of fancy dips and twirls making a slow circle of the dance floor. When we arrived back near her table he mother was standing on the dance floor and cut in. That started a series of cut ins by other women and when I spotted another woman waiting to cut in I would spin my partner off and start dancing with the next one without missing a stride. The orchestra got in the mood and played one waltz after another until, I think, they exhausted their repertoire. The leader then signaled me the last dance before a break and I ended that dance with a big dip. I then escorted the last lady to her table to a resounding round of applause. I then excused myself and left the other two couples, and went home feeling on top of the world. Later in life while courting my wife I took her to the Trianon Ball room in Chicago on Thursday nights which were waltz nights.

Chapter 17

PRANKS

There always has to be an outstanding prank whenever a group of fellows get together and this one I was the butt of. Lt. Sweeting, one of our later replacements, was a person who could smell a cork and pass out. In short, it didn't take much to get him drunk. I on the other hand, seldom drank to excess and when I did, never showed it. One evening Sweeting challenged me to a drinking match and kept pestering me until I finally accepted it and had a few drinks with him until he passed out. About a week later he again challenged me but said the reason he passed out was because he drank mixed drinks and I only had straight shots. This time I had to have a glass of lemonade to chase each shot. Now the lemonade we had was a powdered lemonade and was so strong that nothing else could be tasted except the lemon flavoring. Two pitchers of the mix were used, one for me and one for Sweeting. A glassful of lemonade and a measured shot of whisky was poured in each glass and we chugalugged it. I thought "boy this stuff is hitting me fast." As I reached up to pinch my cheek and could feel neither my hand nor cheek. The guys kept asking me math questions which I managed to answer correctly. Finally Sweeting passed out. We were on our third pitcher at the time and each pitcher must have held at least a fifth of liquid. At that point, I said goodnight gentlemen and proceeded back to my tent very mindful of the tent stakes and ropes that extended beyond the tents. I felt that if I stumbled over one that I might not get up. I successfully got back to my tent and laid down in my bunk at which time my will power gave out and I promptly passed out waking up at three o'clock the next afternoon. Don greeted me with "you damn fool, don't you know what they did. Your lemonade was mixed with pure gin while Sweeting's was mixed with water. They wanted to see you drunk". I replied to the effect that they got their wish but Don protested saying "No they didn't. You acted like you always do and answered all their questions correctly. You didn't even lisp. I wanted to stop it because I thought you might be killed, but they insisted you weren't drunk yet." They may not have realized it but I sure was drunk. That experience may be why I am a teetotaler today. If you don't feel happy or gay when drinking why guzzle the liquor.

Chapter 18

LEAVING BRON

When the Ninth Air Force took over the dive bombing and strafing choirs in France we were once again assigned to the British Eighth Army on the East side of Italy. This was in October of 1944, and we took over a just captured airfield previously occupied by the Germans at Jesi, Italy. It featured a concrete runway 2800 feet in length with a hundred foot circle on each end making a total length of 2900 feet. The P-47s rated takeoff distance was 2800 feet empty, that is without armament, no guns, no rocket tubes, no bombs and no extra fuel tanks. We had all of the above carrying two wing tanks. A five hundred bomb, six rockets and rounds for eight 50 caliber machine guns. The way I took off was to start with only my front wheels on the runway, run the motor up until the brakes wouldn't hold it any more, then release the brakes and push the joy stick forward to lift the tail off the ground, then when I had picked up enough speed, full flaps and pull the stick back to lift the plane in the air, then shove it hard forward to bounce the plane 50 to 70 feet in the air, then pull the stick back to keep it in the air. The plane would start to fall but with no ground resistance started to pick up flying speed quickly and start to climb. I would then slowly close the wing and cowling flaps. In the ten or so missions we flew off the field I never jettisoned my bombs or aborted a takeoff. I can't say that for the rest of the outfit, I had duty one day being stationed in a jeep with Doc Winsaurer at the end of the runway which ended at the beach and the Adriatic Sea. It was one of the scariest days of my life as about 40% of the planes jettisoned their bombs in order to take off. Now the bombs aren't armed and should not explode but there is always the chance that they could be armed if the wire securing their little propeller should be pulled or not properly in place. The propeller unwinds and falls off by the wind current when the wire is pulled. Then the bomb is armed. It seemed like bombs were bouncing past us all day! I only pulled this duty once but it was enough. This was the first time we were armed with rockets. The tubes were bundles of three and we had one group under each wing. Each rocket was equivalent of a 155mm canon shell and all six fired at once. They were deadly and would blow a tank to smithereens. Skip bombing was no longer necessary!

When we were transferred to Jesi the pilots showed up on the 1st of October but the ground crews didn't arrived until seven days later, in the meantime most of the pilots decided to try out the baths in Bano, Italy. Bano means bath and the town was just a little South of Jesi so a short trip South for an honest to goodness bath sounded like a good idea. Don and I checked out a jeep and went for our baths. What we hadn't counted on was that after we were stripped and in the individual concrete tubs a group of women came in armed with scrub brushes and grabbed each of us by the back of the neck and scrubbed our backs until they were red. Then dropped the brushes for us to use and disappeared. I was a little embarrassed but very clean when I left there.

Our job at both Jesi and Fano which we moved to in November was largely close support work in which we used rockets for the first time although we still dive bombed bridges and other targets from time to time. We would have four ship shows and would report in to a ground controller. The shows would be so spaced as to keep near continuous support for the ground troops. We were moveable artillery for them. Anti aircraft on these targets was very heavy. We would start out by reporting in, Commander this is Dickie flight. Do you have a target for us. Dickie flight there is a machine gun nest in the upper floor of the farm house at G-7 on your photo. Do you see it. Roger commander, Wilco. That meant we had it located and would take care of it. Now all six rockets fired at once, and each rocket was like a 105 howitzer shell exploding, a single hit destroyed the whole farmhouse. We would then ask for another target. This was repeated many times, on one occasion a tank went into a barn to hide but when we started down on that barn the tank crew went running as we destroyed the barn and the tank. The results of this close support work were so good the one of the British generals wrote a letter to Colonel Pinkston, our group commander, as follows: "Please accept our grateful thanks and general admiration for the brilliant attacks by your rocket firing Thunderbolts (P-47's). The deadliness and accuracy of your attacks thrilled and stimulated our boys to no ordinary degree. Come up and see us again just as soon as you can."

It was on one such mission after we had shot all of our rockets and had regained altitude for the journey home we were jumped by six ME 109's. By the time I saw them it was almost too late! I told the other three pilots in our squadron to hit the deck as no other fighter could dive as fast a Thunderbolt. I jammed my throttle full forward and turned so sharply in a ninety degree bank I almost grayed out. A gray out is just short of a black out when all the blood rushes out of your head and one loses the ability to see colors, everything appears in black and white. My intent was to protect the tail of the diving aircraft if the German planes tried to follow them down. None did and I found myself in a Luftwaffe circle with the six ME 109's. We weren't supposed to get in a circle with the 109's because they were supposed to be able to turn inside of us but this was not the case. I practically hung that P-47 on its propeller with my wings almost vertical to the ground and turned inside of them. The only problem I had was every time I started shooting the recoil from the guns would start to stall me out so I had to confine myself to very short bursts, give the engine a shot of water and then wait to get in position again to give another short burst. It soon dawned on their leader that he couldn't get a shot on me and if they kept in that circle I was going to shoot the tail off of their last man and they broke the circle and at full throttle headed for home. I immediately thought I'll get all six of them as my plane was slightly faster than theirs and I took a good shot at tail end Charlie. I thought I saw gray smoke come from his plane and he started losing altitude and I started to try and catch up with the next plane. In doing so I glanced at my fuel gage and thought better of it. I throttled back to 1800 r.p.m. and full pitch for maximum fuel efficiency and headed home. I was deep over enemy territory and barely had enough fuel left to get home. If you watched your fuel gage while at full throttle you could actually see the needle of the gauge go down. The engine on a P-47 was an eighteen cylinder two thousand horsepower job, momentary twenty two hundred with water injection. I never did get credit for shooting down an enemy aircraft as there was no confirmation. Evidently the pilot landed it at an emergency field or may even got it back to his base. I got back to base safely but ran out of gas while taxiing to my revetment. That was cutting it close.

Chapter 19

DISTINGUISHED FLYING

On January 31, I was flying yellow leader and my buddy Don was Dickie leader. Don called me on the radio telling me to come down to his flight and take over, he was having engine trouble and had to go back. I immediately called for his element leader to take over yellow flight and I assumed command of the show. Our mission was dive bombing and strafing a railroad yard at Nuklo, Yugoslavia. Trieste, Italy is right on the Yugoslav border and Nuklo was a railroad marshalling about fifty miles from Trieste. We anticipated the flak would be heavy. As we neared the target I spotted a German truck convoy coming out of Trieste. We normally didn't strafe with bombs on

but we needed the bombs for the railroad yard so keeping our bombs on I ordered only Dickie flight to get the first three trucks figuring that would slow them up enough until we took care of the marshalling yard and we could finish them off on our way back. My right wingman was to take the lead vehicle, I would take the second and my left wingman the third. As we pulled off I leaned back against the armor plating and glanced back to see what damage we had done when a heavy caliber bullet took off my oxygen mask and sprayed my chin with plexiglass. I looked at the two holes in the canopy and thought, my God, if I hadn't looked back at that precise moment that bullet would have taken my head off. We had set the first three trucks ablaze. I figured that would hold them for a while, trying to get around those three flaming trucks and proceeded on to our primary target. We then dive bombed the marshalling yard cutting the rail entrance to the Italian border and rocket attacked the trains in the yard. For good measure we machine gunned any locomotives left standing along with quite a few boxcars. As we assembled to leave Kretzer, a wingman in red flight, said he had been hit in the gas tank and wanted to know if he should bail out. From Trieste all the way to Albania the land was covered with deep snow and the Adriatic Sea was grey and white capped. If he bailed out and survived the cold over land he would either be picked up by Michelavich sympathizers and turned over to the Germans or by Tito sympathizers and turned over to the Russians. We had been warned not to ditch in the Adriatic as life expectancy in the cold water was less than twenty minutes and that would not be enough time for the navy to rescue us. All prospects seemed dim. I told him that the tank was self sealing and he should wait until the tank sealed before making a decision. In the meantime he should join up with me and fly alongside setting his prop at full pitch and engine at eighteen hundred r.p.m. for maximum fuel efficiency and that I would set the pace off him. When the tank sealed and he told me how much he had left I made some quick calculations and it seemed like we could come pretty close to landfall. To give us a little margin of safety I put the flight into a very shallow dive, losing about two hundred feet a minute. This picked up our groundspeed slightly and so we could get better mileage. My navigation was good and at one thousand feet of altitude we were looking straight down the runway of the Jesi airfield. I called tower and told them we were coming straight in as I had a wounded bird low on fuel. His windshield was covered with oil and he had opened his canopy half way so that he could see me. I instructed the rest of the flight to assume the normal traffic pattern circling the field until they had landing instruction from the tower. I then guided Kretzer down having him cracking his flaps, then full flaps but not lowering his landing gear until I was sure he could make the runway. I kept him near the edge of the runway so he could use the edge as a steering guide for the landing and at the last second after going through the full landing process, just before I stalled out I gave it the gun and rejoined the rest of the outfit. Kretzer ran out of gas in the middle of the runway and the runway and could not be pulled off before dark. The field had no lights. It was already dusk. We were ordered to land at the fifty-first airfield a little farther South. This was the Tuskegee outfit of the colored airman. After a visit to the officers club and the customary shot and a bull session I was bivouacked with a master sergeant. We discussed race relations for a while after which he concluded I was quite naïve. After the war I was to learn what he was talking about when I was in charge of a carpenter crew on the H-bomb plant at Aiken, South Carolina. I had a habit of placing my hand on a man's shoulder when explaining what I wanted him to do. Now at that time in the early fifties, all the carpenter crews were white but each crew had a laborer and he was always black. I explained to the laborer what I wanted him to do and almost immediately afterwards, one of the carpenters came up to me and said "you treated him as if he were a human being." I said "He is, isn't he?" He answered "No he ain't. He's some sort of monkey." The answer shocked me but I found that this attitude was prevalent amongst the less educated southerners. During the Clinton presidency, one of the sons of a Tuskegee pilot ran for Congress and I donated $50 towards his campaign. I would have loved to have seen him win but he did not. After getting back to our own outfit I found that Kretzer was telling everyone who would listen that I was the smartest pilot in our outfit and that I was coming back alive and he was going to fly my wing for the rest of the war and come back with me. He did fly my wing for several missions but eventually he got promoted and had to assume a more responsible position. I was rewarded the Distinguished Flying Cross for my part in this sortie which read as follows: For extraordinary achievement while participating in aerial flight as pilot of a P-47 type aircraft. On 31 January 1945, Lieutenant Thompson led a ten plane formation of fighter-bombers in an attack upon a marshalling yard at Nuklo, Yugoslavia. Sighting a concentration of motor vehicles upon approach to the target, Lieutenant Thompson dived in attack and destroyed three before a direct hit from enemy ground fire damaged his aircraft and caused flying glass particles to wound him about the face. Despite the intense pain and the crippled condition of his airplane, Lieutenant Thompson, displaying utmost determination and superior leadership, quickly rejoined his formation. Then leading a vigorous bombing and rocket attack against the assigned targets, Lieutenant Thompson and his comrades destroyed or damaged three locomotive and more than twelve freight cars and cutting the rail line in several places. On more than forty five combat missions his outstanding proficiency and steadfast devotion to duty have reflected great credit upon himself and the armed forces of the United States. Signed by John K Cannon, Major General.

What Bull. If I was to get a DFC it should have been for saving a pilot's life or at best, kept him out of a German or Russian prison camp. The Russians, although supposed allies, treated our soldiers as prisoners while attempting to indoctrinate them.

Chapter 20

A WEATHER RECONNAISSANCE

I flew the weather reconnaissance missions for our outfit as I was the best navigator in the 85th squadron. No credit was given for a combat mission on a normal weather recon mission as the purpose of a recon mission was to see if the weather over the target areas was suitable for operations. These flights were usually two ship shows. On this particular flight Kretzer volunteered to be my wingman. It was a day in which there were really two overcasts, one at 18,000 feet above sea level and the other at 2,000 feet above sea level and of varying thickness from 1000 feet to several thousand. We flew up the coast line under the 2000 foot overcast to check on possible enemy activity but there was none. We didn't even attract any ground fire which was unusual when flying that low. The enemy didn't want to give away their locations. Kretzer called out "this is getting downright boring'. I asked him what did he expect on a weather recon. He replied" a little action'. I told him if was action he wanted to tuck it in just behind my wingtip and with his wingtip just a few feet behind my tail section, we would be flying over the clouds and the Austrian Alps. We broke through the clouds at about 28,000 feet then flying at about 30,000 feet until I calculated we were over the Lienz Valley, Austria where we dropped down through the clouds breaking out below the clouds at around two thousand feet. We had barely broken out of the clouds when we spotted two German army trucks on the road just ahead and quickly set them both ablaze with a short burst from our 50 caliber machine guns, the only armament we carried on a weather recon. I then spotted a train to our left going away from us that looked like it was carrying a bunch of empty freight cars. I told Kretzer not to follow as I was going to shoot up the cars from stern to the locomotive in case it was hauling ammunition. It was and when the incendiaries hit the ammo it blew the cars right off the tracks. At the same time all hell broke loose with every anti aircraft battery opening up on us from every direction. There wasn't time to tuck it in and get back in the clouds so I just called out get in the clouds and gave him a bearing to follow on his gyro compass that I knew was safe and he would not run into any mountains. When I did get above the clouds once more it seemed like ages before he broke out many miles to the North and East of me. When I spotted this speck in the sky I slowed down to just above stalling speed and gave him a Southwest bearing to rejoin me. On his own he had no idea of how to get back to base. I had kept track of our position by knowing our direction and the time spent in each direction. When he pulled up alongside he had a huge hole in his right wing. I asked him what had happened and he told me that when the ammo on the train had exploded it put a timber through his wing. I asked him why he had followed when I had told him not to. His reply was I was having all the fun. When I was sure we had cleared the Alps and were once again over the Adriatic Sea he tucked it in and we descended down below the clouds. In retrospect the whole mission was rather foolhardy and should never have been attempted just to satisfy Kretzer's desire to have a little action. To me the war was not fun and games. I viewed it as my duty and when I was in charge it was my duty to inflict as much damage on the enemy as possible and to bring back safely as many of the men in my charge as I could. In leading well over 60 missions I only lost one man and to this day I cannot figure out what I could have done to save that one pilot.

PROPAGANDA

Propaganda is part of any war but it is an unique experience to be the subject of the propaganda. This happened to me during the war. I was leading a four ship show when I spotted a barge carrying two vehicles across a canal and immediately started to attack. As we started down I could see that the rear vehicle was an ambulance with Red Cross markings so I pulled up without firing. As soon as it reached the other side the truck pulled off and disappeared in a camouflaged area on the North side of the canal while the red cross ambulance remained on the barge but was moved up to the front position.

It was obvious that the ambulance was only on the barge to keep us from attacking. I told my element leader to strafe the apparent wooded area on the north side and my wingman to do the same on the south side while I went down on the barge. I was very careful not to hit the ambulance but sank the barge hitting it at the waterline. When it hit bottom the hood of the ambulance was above water. As we left the area smoke was rising from the north side so we must have hit at least one truck. That night we heard on the radio that a pilot flying X-37 had shot up an ambulance carrying a wounded GI aboard. The photos from my gun camera showed that not one bullet from my guns hit the ambulance and besides the British to whom we were attached had charge of the east side of Italy. What would a G.I. have been doing there?

Chapter 21

CASARSUS BRIDGE

We were being briefed on a very hot target, the Casarsus bridge crossing the Udine River. This was a vital link in the German supply line and was heavily defended. Indeed the British had attempted to take it couple of days earlier and had lost seven Spitfires in the attempt. The frame of a Spitfire was balsa wood. It made the Spitfire very maneuverable but also very vulnerable to heavy anti aircraft artillery so the British Command asked the 79th with its rugged P-47s to try and destroy the crossing. We were to have a sixteen ship show. Major Maxwell was to lead. I was to lead yellow flight, the last flight down. Major Maxwell and I belonged to a mutual admiration society. Despite the fact that I had led many shows before he became Company Commander he didn't think I was capable of leading shows and I didn't think he was smart enough to be Company Commander, a fact that I didn't try to hide! As the meeting ended the operational officer asked if there were any questions. I responded asking "what are we going to do about the flak?" intending to explain my idea of using anti personnel bombs against the anti-aircraft batteries. Maxwell said with bravado "We fly right through it, let's go." With that he dashed out the door ending all conversations. We had a late start and arrived over the target in the afternoon, then circled over the target to line up with the railroad tracts diving down on the bridge. In the meantime the German gunners were all primed and started shooting at us before we even started down. Now you may think that it is an easy task to hit the bridge after you line up on the tracks but the bombs do not fall in a straight line but in a parabolic curve from the moment they are release as it would be almost impossible to dive straight down and pull out of such a dive on time so one always had an angle to the earth and had to lead the target. Secondly one has to keep the needle and ball centered (an instrument that shows if one is skidding sideways) while Keeping your gun sight on the tracks. No small task as in a dive your speed quickly builds up to over six hundred miles an hour which in turn increases your torque and one has to practically stand on the left rudder in order to keep the ball centered. All the while shells are exploding all around you. If you release the bomb while still in a skid the bomb also goes sideways. This requires great concentration and good hand and eye coordination. Additionally, an eighty eight shell exploding near you gives the plane a jolt knocking you off line. I changed yellow flights line and started shooting at the gun emplacements with my machine guns to make the gunners duck then change course at the last minute trying to line up quickly to bomb the bridge as did the rest of my flight. This tactic saved yellow flight from casualties but none of us hit the bridge although we came closer that most. Three planes were lost from the other three flights. It was a rather silent group at the debriefing. When the debriefing officer asked if there were any comments I spoke up and said "This was the stupidest mission I was ever on. First we circled the target giving the gunners plenty of time to line up on us, secondly, we came in down sun giving them good visibility for aiming and tracking." Maxwell then piped up saying "If you're so fucking smart, you lead the next show." And with that, he left the room. Mullins, the operations officer, without missing a beat turned to me and asked me how I wished to proceed. I think he had the same idea on Maxwell's competence as I did. I ascertained that we had twelve ships without holes in them and said, "I want the first four ships armed with anti-personnel bombs. I want to arrive over the target at 10 a.m. and come right out of the sun all the way down. We will set our props at one thousand rpm in the dive bomb run so that they will act as brakes and slow down the dive." The railroad tracks ran due east-west. When the anti-personnel bombs started exploding at one hundred feet in the air the gunners had to duck or be hit and didn't recover in time to get an accurate shot even at tail end Charlie. We took the bridge out with no problems with eight direct hits. The anti-personnel bombs were so effective that all three squadrons adopted it as standard procedure and very few planes or pilots were lost thereafter. Maxwell retired shortly thereafter and was replaced by Captain Files who had come overseas as a Captain and had flown my wing while breaking in. Major Fetters who had been CO of the eighty fifth before being transferred to eighty sixth told Files that the reason he put him on my wing was because I was the smartest pilot in the squadron and had never lost a man. Files was promoted to Major and served as Company Commander for the duration. I don't know about being the smartest, but I do know the best way to stay alive was keep you head on a swivel, go straight to the target and always come out of the sun when dive bombing.

Chapter 22

JUST PLAIN LUCKY

We were on our way back after completing our mission of dive bombing and destroying a bridge in Southern France and looking for random targets some tracer bullets passed my right wing. Cussing myself for my carelessness I immediately cracked my flaps causing my plane to rise quickly, then closing my flaps, nosed down and found myself in perfect position to shoot down a ME-109, the mainstay of the German Air Force. However, as I opened fire the plane yawed to the right as only my right outboard gun was firing. I jammed in the left rudder trying to keep the one gun on target. The recoil of a fifty caliber machine gun was too great as it was firing one bullet after another. The ME-109 poured the coal to his craft and with the inertia of his dive pulled away from me. It happened so suddenly none of the other three pilot in our four ship show had spotted the ME 109 either so he got away. After that I took our flight home and on landing I told my crew chief to find out why my other guns hadn't fired. With that said I was off to debriefing and then the officers club. I hadn't been there long before I was summoned to the telephone. It was the military police, they had arrested my crew chief Ed Hollywood and if I wanted him back I would have to come down and sign for his release and take responsibility for him. I immediately grabbed a jeep and went into town where the brig was and had Ed released to my custody. Ed had checked my guns and found out that only the first gun had been cocked. It seems that the armorer in his rush to go on leave had failed to initially cock the other seven guns! Ed then went into town to the bar where he knew the armorer hung out and had with a series of punches, knocked him out. You can see the reason why I found the fact that the armorer outranked the crew chief intolerable when I first got my own plane. The next day I only said two words to the armorer, "lesson learned." Evidently the German pilot did not have his needle and ball centered so he was in a slight skid making him miss me to the right. I thanked the Lord for that and I got to live another day.

OUTCLASSED

We were on a routine dive bombing mission of a bridge in the Northern Po Valley. We had an eight ship show, I was Dickie leader and Frank Ward was yellow leader. I always enjoyed those shows where Frank was my yellow flight leader as we usually had some light hearted banter along the way. We knew that Jerry monitored our conversations so in our best Hebrew accents we would talk. I addressed him as Wardenstein and he address me as Thompson burger. It might not have seemed so funny had we known of Auschwitz at that time but we didn't and we did know of Hitler's hatred of the Jews. It was just a couple of Irishmen taunting Hitler. At any rate we were bombing a bridge crossing the Adage River and after I had dropped my bombs was recording the hits and misses on my knee pad when Frank coming off his run yelled in his microphone "Thompson, there's a twin engine job on your tail!" Breaking sharply to the right followed by diving to the left I opened fire on an aircraft with German markings giving him a three ring lead. Got him I thought as thick black smoke came out of his engines. Then a strange thing happened, instead of going down he rapidly pulled away from me. What the devil! I must be stalled. I glanced at my airspeed indicator and saw it was indicating in excess of two Hundred m.p.h. When we returned to base I reported the incident in my debriefing and the operation officer promptly sent for the film in my gun camera. It seems I had been jumped by a ME 262 jet aircraft. My first few bullets had gone into the tail section, the rest were behind the jet. The smoke I saw was when he poured the coal to the burners and took off. It was the first sighting of a German Jet in the Italian theatre. A week later, Don was also jumped by a German jet, probably the same one.

Chapter 23

MAJOR FILES

Major Files was giving a briefing on the status of the war effort when he was interrupted by a telephone call. Major Files had come overseas as a Captain and had been assigned to fly my wing to get some experience before he started leading shows. He took over as squadron commander when Maxwell left. The telephone call was from the British Eighth field headquarters and he responded by saying into the phone no, we have no one by that name then turning to the assembled group he asked "anyone here know of a Van Hooten or Howten?" Don Lawless and I jumped up simultaneously shouting Van. We then explained his name was Eugene Van Houten and he, Don and I had all come overseas together. Files told us to grab a jeep and go to British Eighth field headquarters and identify him as we were the only ones left that knew him. The British were skeptical that he was an American pilot because sometimes he didn't know the proper English word and would lapse into Italian. On reaching the field headquarters Van was waiting there and rushed to greet us. After some jovial rounds of back slapping we starting asking him how he escaped being caught by the Germans and staying with the Italian partisans for over a year. We then discovered that being with the Italian partisans in constant fear of being caught had taken its toll on him as he continuously asked me in Italian for the proper English word to express himself. I spoke fairly good Italian at that time having taken two years of Latin when I was in high school. Don never did pick up the language. He told us how an Italian family had taken him in and on occasion he went into town with a teen age girl and they would or at least she would banter with the German soldiers saying Van was her boy friend. At any rate we took him back to our outfit where they debriefed him for a few days and then at his choice flew three more missions. This would not have been possible had he been picked up by the Germans. After that the war was over and we shut down operations. The three Musketeers were together again. We had gone all the way through cadet training together and overseas to the same outfit. It looked like we would all go home together. However for some ungodly reason we all came back separately. I might say however that speaking Italian stood me in good stead on occasions when I became City Engineer in Roseville, California. Most of the residents were of an Italian background and some did not speak good English. In trying to explain an assessment district for street paving and curbs and sidewalk to a woman by her house, she did not understand the English, so I did my best at explaining it in Italian. When I finished she was all smiles saying "you great engineer, you speak Italian." After that I could do no wrong in her eyes.

On an occasion later in my tour of duty when I was stationed at Fano, Italy I was to accompany Doc Winsauer on a jeep trip to Naples and pick up a replacement aircraft and fly that aircraft back to Fano. The trip back to base was on a beautiful day and I decided to do a few acrobatics on the way staring with a barrel roll to the right. When I had completed it I thought the left wing was at a slightly different angle then when I started. Then just to make sure I carefully marked where the leading edge of the wing was on my fuselage I made a barrel roll in the opposite direction. The position of the wing changed back to where I had thought it originally should have been. Holy Cow! The left wing was not securely fastened. How glad was I that I hadn't' started with a slow roll where the wing might have broken off when I was upside down. I flew straight and level the rest of the way at reduced air speed. When I arrived at base I taxied to my revetment where I asked Ed Hollywood, my crew chief to take a look at that left wing and see what was wrong.

We took the wing off and found that only one bolt had been holding the wing on when there should have been six. I reported this to Major Files and before I could leave his office he had the replacement depot on the Phone and was giving them hell about there lack of inspection on the aircraft before they released it. All I can say is there must have been someone up there looking out for me.

"anyone here know of a Van Hooten or Howten?" Don Lawless and I jumped up simultaneously shouting Van. We then explained his name was Eugene Van Houten and he, Don and I had all come overseas together.

E. T. Van Houten, F. J. Waice and K. A. Thompson

Files told us to grab a jeep and go to British Eighth field headquarters and identify him as we were the only ones left that knew him. On reaching the field headquarters Van was waiting there and rushed to greet us. After some jovial rounds of back slapping we starting asking him how he escaped being caught by the Germans and

Chapter 24

DOWN BEHIND ENEMY LINES

Some people seem to think it was a great feat getting back to our outfit after being shot down behind enemy lines. At the time I was shot down it really wasn't that difficult. It was near the end of the war, the Germans were in full retreat trying to get back to Germany to defend the motherland. Although technically it was enemy held territory it was really occupied land and most of the Italians were friendly. Rural Italians were almost 100% pro American. If one understood the German method of hunting for downed pilots and I did, it was merely remaining out of sight for the first two hours. They would throw a circle around your downed plane about a mile in diameter and search the interior of the circle. If they didn't find you they enlarged the circle based on how far you could walk in the elapsed time and kept expanding it as time passed. I went under a bridge near the abutment, from the middle of abutment I walked at a 90 degree angle to the water. Then back tracking to the abutment swung up on the I beams and crawled out to where I was twelve to fifteen feet above the ground. This is something I had done as a young boy in River Falls, Wisconsin. My step brother and I, Floyd Henderson by name, used to crawl out to the center piers on the bridge over the Kinikinick River to gather young pigeons before they could fly, then raise them for squab meat. My back hurt me as I had banged it in the course of the crash landing, later I found out I had cracked a few vertebras. A German soldier with a dog passed underneath and abandoned the search figuring I had gone in the water. The dog however , kept pointing at the abutment and I held my breath but the soldier paid no attention and jerked on his leash pulling the dog away and continued upstream. After a couple of hours I dropped down and started walking on rural roads in a general southerly direction. I took off my flying suit as I had civvies underneath. I even stayed in the dirt cellar of an empty farm house when our planes were bombing a nearby bridge and shared it with two German soldiers. I was sitting on my flying suit. They said something to me in German and I answered in Italian "non parlata Tedesco" which meant I didn't speak German. They left when the bombing stopped and I left shortly after. I think they were deserters. I kept my flying suit rolled up and used it at night for warmth. I ate dried onions like apples and was given some bread and tomatoes by friendly farmers. My biggest disappointment was when I got back to my outfit and found my collection of hand carved pipes had been dispersed. It took a few days but I eventually got most of them back. I had a figure of Christ with the wreath forming the top of the bowl, a tennis ball on a racket with the top of the ball cut to form a bowl and several animal head pipes. Eventually they were all stolen but that happened here in the States.

Chapter 27

THE 97ᵀᴴ MISSION

My 97ᵗʰ mission was to be dive bombing a restaurant in the Austrian Alps. I was told I was chosen for this mission because of my ability to conserve gas on long missions and this mission was fairly close to the maximum range for a P-47 when carrying a five hundred pound bomb. My first question was "What is the military significance of this target?" Hitler once dined there I was told. My next question was, "Is he there now?" "No, he is in Berlin." "Then what is the military significance?" No answer. I continued, "You know these bombs are known to kill people and I didn't sign on in this war to kill a bunch of cooks and waitress or diners either for that matter." The operations officer went on to say ".ell, we are just trying to get you guys a hundred missions." I then said that getting a hundred missions didn't mean that much to me especially if it meant bombing a bunch of civilians. I would take any military target, but there was no point in destroying anything unnecessarily just to get a hundred missions. At the time I said this, only Don Lawless and I of the pilots active at that time had over ninety missions. The records show that eleven pilots ended up with exactly 100 missions and more that that had over ninety. However, I had made my point. No more buildings were considered for targets and the restaurant was removed from the list. I flew no more missions. Where those bombs were dropped to give those other guys one hundred missions I do not know. When I brought the matter up with Don he agreed with me, but went on the purported mission and dropped his bombs in the Adriatic. To this day I imagine there are quite a few unexploded bombs on the bottom of the Adriatic Sea.

Chapter 28

THE TRIP HOME

Major Files called me into his office (a tent) and explained he was staying on in the army of occupation and asked me if I would stay on also and be his second in command. It would mean a promotion to Captain for me. I declined saying I was no peacetime army officer. After a short discussion he asked me to turn in my watch and gun. The next day I was interviewed by another officer from operations who told me flatly I had too many points to be shipped back by boat and that they were going to fly me home. Points were figured on the basis of days overseas, medals won, campaigns participated in and what have you. He actually called me a hero. I was quite flattered. I assumed Don Lawless would be going back with me as he had as many points as I, although he had one less Air Medal and other than that our records would be identical. Not so, Don told me afterward he was not interviewed and only the Army could figure out why. I was promptly shipped to a replacement depot in Naples where on that evening I, with the company of many other officers had one hell of a drunk including the Colonel in charge of the port. I hit the sack sometime between one and two a.m. with my head reeling only to be awakened by an enlisted man about three thirty a.m. and informed I was on guard duty as the officer of the guard. I very groggily got up, didn't shave and didn't notice the shirt I put on had no insignia. I was delivered to the post by jeep and relieved the current officer of the guard and we posted the new guard and he passed on his instructions to me. I wondered why we even had a guard, it seemed pointless. The G.I.'s were all on leave so we weren't checking any passes and the Italian civilians walked right through the warehouse which was straddling the street. At any rate I started playing pinochle with some of the fellows. About 9 a.m. in comes the Officer of the Day, a Captain, all spit and polish and obviously had just arrived in Naples on a troop transport that was still in the harbor. His first question was "who was the Officer of the Guard?" No one shouted attention when he came in and we all continued playing cards, very unmilitary. Without getting up I said I was. He then asked me to step outside where he asked me my rank. When I told him 1st Lt. he seemed to breathe a sigh of relief and ordered me to go back to the barracks, shave and put on some insignia after which we would inspect the guard. When we inspected the guard none of the enlisted men on guard duty knew how to make a rifle salute although I stood behind the Officer of the Day and tried to imitate a rifle salute, but their attempts left a lot to be desired. None of them had carried a rifle in their entire stay overseas. They all had been mechanics, armorers, clerks or kitchen personnel. When we finished he started to give his opinion but I stopped him and told him the soldiers on duty were a bunch of mechanics and armorers who hadn't had a rifle in their hands in over 2 years of overseas duty and that he had just got off the boat, had seen no combat duty and that he had no idea of what these men had been through, and further more this was a useless guard duty and should be abandoned, and that I was going to take it up with Colonel Johnson at noon. He said I was probably right but he would take it up with the Colonel not me. I then suggested he wait until noon because the Colonel probably had a hell of a hangover. When he asked me how I was certain he had a hangover I told him because I was with him the night before and I knew how much he had drunk. He was shocked to find out that a Colonel would be associating with lower ranks but overseas not much attention was paid to normal protocol. We all had a job to do and we did it. At any rate the guard was disbanded except for four men at the warehouse which contained mattresses and nothing else and these were burned after we left. I didn't see the Officer of the Day again and I stayed on until the end of the shift. The following day I took a plane to Tunis in North Africa where I spent one more week before flying home. I did get some flying time in which was the only break from boredom. The plane home was a four engine job loaded with state department personnel from all over the mid east and a few military men like myself. I sat next to a secretary from the Egyptian consulate who had a small chess set in her purse and we played several games to pass the time. We arrived in Bermuda after dark and stayed overnight. It was pitch black out and the Island was under a blackout. We left before dawn and although I can truthfully say I was in Bermuda I have no idea what the island looked like or even the lobby of the hotel we stayed at. New York was fogged in and we circled the field (La Gardia) for over five hours (we had refueled in Bermuda so we were at the bottom of the list for instrument landing clearance). The system used was all planes coming in were at two thousand foot intervals from two thousand feet to twenty eight thousand feet. Every time the lowest plane landed the others were told to drop down two thousand feet. Because we had refueled in Bermuda we had plenty of gas and were sent back to the top several times. We circled for over five hours before we received clearance to land. Once we landed I called up my crew chief's (Ed Hollywood) wife, which I had promised to do and gave her a short visit, she lived in Brooklyn. The streets of Brooklyn stunk. The garbage hadn't been picked up for two weeks due to a strike by their patriotic collectors. The next day I was on a plane to Los Angeles where Don Lawless met me and informed me he had set us up for that evening with a couple of Hollywood starlets. Naturally he had the nice girl, mine was an egocentric gal that thought she was god's gift to creation. She proved that by going up to the Maitre de and insisted he put us at the head of the line for a table at one of Hollywood's exclusive dining places. Standing in line were several big name stars that I recognized including Cary Grant, Van Johnson and quite frankly I had never heard of her. I was embarrassed! Needless to say, after dinner I said the flight had bushed me and dropped her off and returned to our barracks. Don didn't get in until the wee hours. I would rather have gone fishing in John Wayne's boat which was available!

I took a side trip to see my dad who was an instructor at Thunderbird Airfield in Arizona where he took me up in a training plane and asked me to perform. It was quite different from flying a two thousand horsepower fighter where maneuvers required only a small pressure on the joy stick compared to a less than two hundred horsepower trainer and where you moved the rudder and stick quite visibly to get movement. However I did a passable job. When it came time to land he motioned he would take the controls and as we were landing with the power off, did a slow roll in which the wing tip cleared the ground buy less than three feet but still made a perfect three point landing then stood with a grin on his face as I gave my best performance of chewing a cadet out for pulling a risky maneuver so close to the ground. After which we both laughed and enjoyed each other's company. I then took a troop train to Chicago where I was discharged on September 7, 1945 and reentered Illinois Institute of Technology where as a returning student I receive priority and got right back in. If you weren't a returning student there was a two year waiting list. I also changed my major from mechanical to civil engineering. I changed it because in flying over the coastlines of France and Italy I had observed that the coastlines were brown from sewage all the way from Spain to Naples and beyond and that the public drinking fountains were not always safe. I was entitled to four years under the GI Bill, one month for every month of service and I took full advantage of it training myself for a management position in Public works. I earned over one hundred and ninety credit hours broadening my knowledge horizontally rather than getting a masters degree. I could have had a degree in Political science or in Social Science or Civil Engineering, Management option and chose the later because the school would only give one degree at a time. I served as a class president, vice president of the student body and an editor on the school newspaper in addition to sports. It earned me some recognition being named to Who's Who in American Colleges and Universities. I also met my future wife at a dance there which lasted 57 years until she died in October, 2006.

Chapter 27

EPILOGUE

For those of us who lived through the war a common expression was "It's an experience I wouldn't take a million dollars for but wouldn't give a plugged nickel to do it again." So true, war is hell, the devastation and human tragedy is terrific and getting worse all the time but it is sometimes necessary. Principle is the only thing worth fighting for. Freedom is one of those principles. There will always be those individuals like Stalin, Hitler and the radical Muslim clerics who love power and hold it ruthlessly. We as Americans are fortunate to live under the greatest Constitution ever devised by man. It has made this Country great and the envy of the world. O'Reilly, a commentator on Fox news says we are a Christian Country founded on Christian principles. This is not quite true. We are a Country founded by Christians based on the principles of John Locke's theory of natures laws. John Adams, our second president and a fiery advocate of independence accused Jefferson, our third president and the writer of the Constitution of stealing the thoughts of John Locke when writing the Constitution. Our forefathers came to this country in order to worship god in the manner they saw fit, they were Pilgrims, Anglicans, Calvinists, Catholics and others and got along with each other fine and they liked it that way. They wanted no government tithing supporting a church as King George's England did, Spain did and Richelieu's France did. They figured everyone should worship in their own way at the church of their choice supported only by their own parishioners. That is why we have in the Constitution a declaration that the government shall adopt no religion. It left us all free to adopt our own. It merely says our government shall adopt no religion, not that we as individual shall be free from religion. The writers assumed that we as individuals would have our own religions based on the Ten Commandments and therefore be of good moral character. The

Supreme Court has in my opinion overstepped when they outlawed the Ten Commandments because it is a part of the Hebrew religion. Seven of the Ten Commandments are rules by which any society must live by if it is to exist for more than one generation. Honor thy mother and father, don't steal, don't commit murder, don't commit adultery, don't covet thy neighbor's wife or possessions, and don't bear false witness. These are nothing more than rules for a successful society and should be taught in every public school in the country. A seventh, keep holy the Sabbath is a physical and mental necessity and should be interpreted as a day of rest and relaxation. It is a time for thought and the meaning of life. Man has worshipped a god or gods since his very beginning and it has usually been his explanation for things he could not understand. Lincoln, our sixteenth president and in my opinion our greatest, once observed that he could understand how a man on the moon looking down on earth could be an atheist but he could not understand how a man on earth looking up at the heavens could not believe in God. I have often gazed at the heavens on a clear night seeing billions of stars, countless galaxies, and realizing that this planet earth is like a pebble of sand on a beach and wondering what started all this and coming to a conclusion that there must be a God. I also recall a phrase of a famous atheist that proves my point; "I do not believe in God but I sleep better at night knowing my neighbor does."

Massachusetts was the first State to adopt a public schooling system as it recognized that education is necessary to promote good citizenship. Other States were quick to follow seeing the benefits of an educated society. The Federal government got involved on the theory that some states were richer than others and could therefore have a better schooling system than poorer states so to level the playing field they got involved to distribute the wealth equally. Like every other thing the government gets into it has done a damn poor job with the Supreme Court making decisions that it had no business getting into. The two biggest mistakes the Supreme Court has made in recent years are the rulings on the separation of Church and State and on Freedom of Speech. Justice Thurgood Marshall ruled a long time ago that there are limits to freedom of speech, Language contrary to the norms and mores of the majority of our populace should not be on our airways. The Federal government should only be concerned with our national defense, protecting our borders, interstate commerce, and relations with foreign countries. This is the way our Constitution was written and the sooner we get back to it the better off we will be.

Our schools, big city schools, are graduating youngsters who can no longer read, add, subtract, multiply or divide. They do not know who Adam, Madison or Monroe are. They do not know we are a Republic, not a Democracy and thank God that we are a Republic and not a Democracy. They know all about women's rights but don't realize that those would be lost if we lose the war against Muslim fundamentalist in Iraq and Afghanistan. Too many of our teachers do not know what the Koran says and are using the classroom to rail against the war. Our so called shortage of teachers is actually a shortage of math and science teachers which could be cured by paying math and science teachers more. This would get more students to realize that the tougher courses pay more. When all teachers are paid the same, why take on the tougher courses? We now have as many administrators in the school systems as teachers. The large school districts were supposed to save money by increasing the buying power and saving money through large purchases. This has not been accomplished. Any savings that might have been in the buying is lost in the distribution costs and the increased numbers of administrators are a big cost for which there is no return. In my day each school had its citizen's board, the principle was the administrator and substitute teacher and we had a teacher for each grade. Discipline was good and enforced by each teacher. An errant student had to hold out his hand palm up and received a resounding whack with a flat ruler. Talking back to a teacher was taken care of by the parents or guardian by the use of a belt or willow stick. No one got away with talking back or disrespecting the teacher. We need some changes! Long ago Chief Justice Marshall ruled that there were limits to freedom of speech yet we see that in the name of free speech, language on the airways that is contrary to the norms and mores of the general populations, college professors can teach sedition and solutions to the race problems like kill the whites! This is ridicules! Wake up Supreme Court. These are the seeds of self destruction. Is this what we fought for? How did we get this way?

Chapter 28

AFTER THOUGHTS

The 14th Amendment to the Constitution says "All persons born or naturalized in the United States, and subject to the jurisdiction thereof, are citizens of the United States and of the State wherein they reside. The intent of this amendment was that all the slaves after the emancipation were citizens. It was never intended that foreigners, here legally or not, would be citizens as they were still citizens of another country and subject to the jurisdiction of that country and therefore do not meet the intent of this amendment. Somehow or other this amendment has been misinterpreted to mean that anyone born in the United States is automatically a citizen. We cannot afford to continue to give these people free education, medical care and food stamps. A hospital cannot turn anyone away for emergency services and the illegal have taken full advantage of this and our humanitarian laws and do not pay their bills. More than one hospital has had to close the doors because of this. We need a bill from Congress clarifying this.

ON MUSLIM TOLERANCE

At times we seem to be leaning over backwards for the Muslims in this country our own federal government suing a school district on behalf of a Muslim teacher who wanted a three week leave of absence to visit Mecca when the school district would only grant her two weeks. It is the most intolerant religion of all the major religions, you are either a true believer or an infidel, women have few rights and if you don't believe that, read Nonie Darwish's book "The Joys of a Muslim woman". Under Sharia law woman are not educated, must wear a burka, can be whipped in public for exposing their ankles or face and should be killed if they

71

leave their religion. For some reason we keep trying to give Muslim nations democratic governments when we really should mean republics, when in truth their very religion makes it improbable. It is highly unfortunate that our form of government is so often call Democratic. It is not! Democracy is mob rule. We have a Republic, a rule of law where minority rights are respected and protected. We elect representative by Democratic vote for representatives to act on our behalf within those laws. Sharia law, which some of our judges say apply, are against our constitution and anyone advocating it should be deported! One thing is certain, Muslims who believe in Sharia law do not believe in our form of government and are no friend of the U.S.A.

OIL

The price of gasoline at the pump has doubled in the two years Obama has been president and it looks as if it will go higher. He has consistently not spoken the truth about the amounts of petroleum and gas available here in the United States. We have more oil in reserves then Saudi Arabia. The shale oils in the Williston basin (Montana, North and South Dakota) alone have enough oil for two hundred years at our present consumption rate and there is a government report that confirms this. This does not include Alaska or our coastal waters or other interior areas which contain oil. We are being held hostage to the idea of green energy. Until oil goes over $150 to $250 a barrel wind, solar, tidal and geothermal are not even closely competitive with natural gas, clean coal energy or hydro power. Why is it alright for us to pay for Brazil through the International Monetary Fund to deep sea drill for oil and not do it ourselves. It is time we stopped sending money overseas creating jobs elsewhere and develop our own resources and jobs. Solution-Drill baby drill!

MONEY AND BANKING

Over 200 years ago, Thomas Jefferson, The writer of the Declaration of Independence and our 3rd president warned that "If the American people ever allow the private banks to control their currency, first by inflation, then by deflation, then the banks and the corporations that will grow up around the banks will deprive the people of all property until their children wake up homeless in the continent their fathers conquered."

We have recently experienced the housing inflation and deflation and we must not permit it to happen again. The housing market will take several years to recover. Barney Franks and Christopher Dodd, with be best of intentions, however not realistic, (the road to hell is paved with good intentions), introduced in Congress a nothing down payment for the purchase of homes. Fannie May and Freddie Mac were also created to guarantee these loans. The private banks now had nothing to lose, they could sell their mortgages to Freddy and Fannie and qualify anybody through small interest loans and balloon payments pocketing the closing costs or interest if any. We see what happened. They also gambled with our money, when successful they were geniuses, and rewarded generously. The banks dealt in billions and the rewards were in millions. We saw many leverage buyouts. Buyout specialists would examine the books of profitable companies with little or no debt, make a bid at over the average price per share with borrowed money until they had a controlling interest, take over management at inflated salaries, and mortgage the company to pay back the leveraged loan. These transactions benefit no one except the buyout specialists and the banks. This practice should be stopped and the big banks should be broken up! They concentrate too much money!

THE UNITED NATIONS

The dream of a one world where all nations lived in peace was and is an utopian dream but not a very realistic one. We and a few others are so far ahead of the rest of the world in a standard of living there is no comparison. Perhaps half the people in this world live under dictatorships, not parliamentary democracies or republics where rights of minorities are protected. Free trade agreements immediately put our workers in competition with the Chinese coolie or other underpaid workers of the world. The manipulation of the currencies of other nations has made us a debtor nation and our economy subject to the World Trade Organization. We should not be seeking free trade agreement, what we need is equal trade agreements. Our soldiers who swear to uphold the Constitution of the United States should never be forced to wear the insignia of the United Nations. Our soldier, I believe his name was Michael New, should be given an Honorable discharge and no American soldier should ever again be forced to serve under any other flag but our own. We pay too much of the costs of the United Nations, the money would be better used to serve our own interests.

Ken Thompson

THE UTILITIES

Most utility companies are publicly owned stock share companies with boards of directors elected by the share holders. Their rates are subject to a public utility commission usually appointed by the governor of the state. This is because the company is granted and exclusive franchise free of competition. Because they have a guaranteed rate of return only two things are necessary for good management, good accounting and good engineering. There is excellent job security, health benefits and retirement benefits in working for these companies and all the costs are borne by the consumers of the services provided. They usually have very large boards of director in the name of having diversification and pay these people handsomely. It is a nice place to park the husband or wife of a key politician who can do them favors. Twenty man boards are not uncommon, and as such would be unworkable if they were actively running the company but the real work is done by a committee of five or seven and the rest just show up once or twice a year all at the cost of the consumer. Southern California Edison is typical, pays its CEO over $8,000,000 per year plus bonuses, has two assistants at over $4,000,000. Of course, these are part of the utilities expenses, and entitles the utility to pass these costs on along with their benefits plus the guaranteed rate of return, usually around 11%. In my opinion the pay should be about half that and the number of paid board outside directors should not exceed eleven and their salary should not exceed a salary of $1000 per meeting. Start attending those rate hearings of your State.

UNIONS

I am not against unions, in the 1930's they performed a necessary function. They still can perform a useful function in negotiations for salaries of workers but I am against national unions with their mafia like tactics which we certainly saw in Wisconsin. The problem with unions of government workers was for the most part that no one represented the taxpayer. Politicians eager for the votes of a large block of voters would not oppose union demands. This has lead to overreaching by the unions, not so much in the field of salaries, although they were getting there, but in the area of benefits which were more hidden until these unfunded liabilities reached the point of breaking the government entities. This is why benefits beyond a retirement of 50% of your last 3 year salary average should be off limits for negotiations.

74

WAGES, BONUSES AND TAXES

We, living in the United States of America, under the protection of our constitution and the Republican form of government, are the most fortunate people on earth. To keep it that way we must be eternally vigilant. We are straying too far from the concepts of our founding fathers! Competitive Capitalism gives more benefits to the multitudes than any other economic form. Karl Marx admitted this in his book the Communist Manifesto but what he foresaw as the end result was not competitive capitalism but laize faire capitalism which meant "no holds barred ". The big would swallow up the small and the worker would work for less and less in the name of competiviness. To a degree we are seeing this today as administrative salaries are becoming too large, receiving too large of a percentage of the profits of their respective companies. I do not understand this mindset, no supervisor is any better than the team he has working for him and without their cooperation could not accomplish anything. As a director of public works I once turned down a raise when the City Council offered me a 25% raise because of the improvements I had brought about while refusing the raises I had recommended for the men. I gave notice of my departure. At the next meeting the men got their raise, I got mine and my resignation was not accepted. Bonuses should be team bonuses. I do not understand the Republican Party reluctance to put a temporary surtax on these overpaid individuals. They personally do not create jobs, businesses create jobs. Bonuses should also be subject to the same surtax when excessive unless they are shared down the line. The money derived from this could be used to lower the business tax to 28% or pay down the National debt. A payroll tax of 0.5% on those earning over $400,000 and 1% on those over a million would not hurt the recovery one bit. On the inheritance tax (sometimes called the death tax), I would favor an exemption of the first five million but have a 25% tax thereafter. This would protect family businesses and farms but would not let the billionaires off the hook. Very few of these muti-millionaires and billionaires have ever paid the proper percentage of their income. They always find or create loopholes.

Ken Thompson

SUMMARY

It looks like Paul Ryan, Republican Congressman, has come up with a workable plan to cut the spending deficits by 6 trillion over ten years but it is still not enough to give us a balanced budget. Why not add the payroll surtax to this with the money going to reduce the deficit and see if we can come up with a balance budget within ten years. The reductions in spending are the priority and the surtax should not be used to offset the spending cuts!!!

For those people who do not wish to see Social Security changed so their children and grandchildren can have the same benefits we now have, forget it! When Social Security was first formed life expectancy for men was 68 and for women 70. Today life expectancy is in the 80s and rising. There will not be enough people under 65 to support those over 65 without confiscatory Social Security tax increases. The same goes for Medicare, Medicare costs must be within our ability to pay. Democracies last only as long as they do not add more benefits than they can pay for!!!